America I AM

Exhibit

America I AM: *The African American Imprint* is a touring museum exhibition that celebrates four hundred years of African American contributions to the nation through artifacts, documents, multimedia, photographs, and music. The exhibition presents a historical continuum of pivotal moments in courage, conviction, and creativity that solidifies the undeniable imprint of African Americans across the nation and around the world.

• ● •

Praise for the

America I AM

The African American Imprint

"This exhibit is beyond words . . . There were times during the tour that I felt myself swelling with so much pride it felt like fire inside . . ."

". . . One of the best cultural experiences of my life . . . I am proud. I am inspired. I am changed."

". . . It tells our history from the start to now with dignity and truth . . ."

". . . An exhibit that should not be missed by any American."

America I AM

Pass It Down Cookbook

Also by
Jeff Henderson

Cooked: My Journey from the Streets to the Stove

Chef Jeff Cooks: In the Kitchen with America's Inspirational Culinary Star

Also by
Ramin Ganeshram

Sweet Hands: Island Cooking from Trinidad and Tobago

Stir It Up!

America I AM
Pass It Down Cookbook

Jeff Henderson

WITH

Ramin Ganeshram

SMILEYBOOKS

Distributed by

HAY HOUSE, INC.

Carlsbad, California • New York City
London • Sydney • Johannesburg
Vancouver • Hong Kong • New Delhi

© 2011 by Tavis Smiley

Published in the United States by: SmileyBooks, 250 Park Avenue South, Suite 201, New York, NY 10003 • **www.SmileyBooks.com**

Distributed in the United States by: Hay House, Inc.: www.hayhouse.com • *Published and distributed in Australia by:* Hay House Australia Pty. Ltd.: www.hayhouse.com. au • *Published and distributed in the United Kingdom by:* Hay House UK, Ltd.: www. hayhouse.co.uk • *Published and distributed in the Republic of South Africa by:* Hay House SA (Pty), Ltd.: www.hayhouse.co.za • *Distributed in Canada by:* Raincoast: www.raincoast.com • *Published and Distributed in India by:* Hay House Publishers India: www.hayhouse.co.in

Design: Charles McStravick • *Indexer:* Therese Shere
Interior photos and illustrations: Credits in text

Grateful acknowledgment is made to all of our America I AM *Pass It Down Cookbook* contributors who generously shared their recipes, essays, photos, and love.

Library of Congress Control Number: 2010940269

Tradepaper ISBN: 978-1-4019-3135-3
Digital ISBN: 978-1-4019-3136-0

14 13 12 11   5 4 3 2
1st edition, February 2011
2nd edition, February 2011

Printed in the United States of America

"African Americans planted it, grew it, harvested it, cooked it, served it . . ."

— Jessica B. Harris

Iron Pots & Wooden Spoons:
Africa's Gifts to New World Cooking

PORK CHOP & EGGS
BACON & EGGS ~~~
HAMBURGER STEAK & EGGS
SAUSAGE & EGGS
SHORT RIBS & MACARONI 2
BEEF STEW & RICE ~~ 2
EGGS & GRITS ~~~
HOT CAKES ~~~ 15
HASH & RICE ~~~ ~~

Contents

Preface

Maya Angelou once shared a childhood memory with me that high-lighted the significant role food has played in the lives of African Americans since the beginning of slavery through today. I still can't believe that I had the privilege of sharing such a special moment with the great poet, civil rights activist, American icon, and celebrated cook.

It was a spring morning in 2009 when I was preparing myself for what I imagined would be one of the most spiritually enriching interviews of my life. The venue: "Grand-mother's Kitchen." The topic: What food means to black folks. Not being a scholar or historian, I knew what food meant to my family and me, but I wasn't certain I was well informed enough about the history of soul food to discuss it in a meaningful way with the woman that the famous food writer M.F.K. Fisher called "one of the ten best cooks she ever met."

Although we were conducting the interview by phone, I was still nervous as I waited for her on the line. I had been on TV countless times and worked with numerous celebrities, but there was something intimidating and incredibly special about being interviewed by Maya. Finally, the phone rang. Hello, Chef Jeff," I replied, hoping she couldn't sense how nervous I was. Then I heard her incredibly distinct, melodious, and powerful voice—commanding and humble at the same time—and somehow I felt at ease.

Maya started the conversation by telling me about her grandmother and how much she loved and admired her. More than anyone else in her life, Maya felt indebted to her grandmother because she was the person that helped form her deep connection with food. Her intimate descriptions of her grandmother in the kitchen and her food philosophy felt magical to me. She explained how her grandmother always kept a pot of rice on the stove when she was a little girl and what that pot meant to her.

Maya's memories transported me back in time. My mind raced back to the late 60s and early 70s when my sister and I would visit our grandparents' home (on 77th Street in Los Angeles) nearly every weekend and on every holiday.

My grandparents' cooking had its roots in New Orleans, with a bit of Alabama thrown in—where my grandfather, Charles Henderson, was born and raised. Even though we all lived in Los Angeles when I was growing up, what was cooked in my grandparents' kitchen never really strayed far from their true roots. When we were over for dinner they'd set large platters of crispy fried chicken, chicken 'n' dumplings, smothered pork chops, stuffed bell peppers, and hot link sandwiches on the table, along with traditional side dishes like slow-cooked collard greens seasoned with ham hocks, lima beans, cabbage cooked with rendered bacon, string beans with salt pork, candied yams, red beans and rice, black-eyed peas, and macaroni and cheese. This type of cooking has been called *"soul food,"* first by African Americans in the United States and finally by others around the world.

Over the decades, soul food has changed in many ways—with even the very name of the cuisine becoming a subject of debate. While few would likely argue that soul food is exclusive to African Americans, the fact that our traditional dishes are now being featured as "Southern cuisine" strikes many as an ironic twist. While many of these foods are commonly prepared in the Southern states, this type of cooking has never been limited to a single region—not during slavery and certainly not today. There are, however, some very unique local versions of the cuisine that do represent African American foodways specific to certain regions, like Low Country cooking that spans the Carolinas, Caribbean soul in Florida, Creole in Louisiana, and so on.

My dining experiences around the country have brought me to the conclusion that every region in America has its own take on soul food. I've reached deep into my Louisiana roots for the inspiration that defines my own approach to soul food, which I call Posh Urban Cuisine. It's a California-French style combined with African American flavors and ingredients. I'm a classically trained chef but my love of Southern cuisine is still an important part of who I am, and that's why you'll find a soulful signature on any plate of food that I serve you.

Similarly, the America I AM *Pass It Down Cookbook* is filled with recipes that reflect the generations-long need to document and share our history and culture. As African American people, it is imperative that we record our culinary contribution to America's kitchen. The recipes in this book are accompanied by personal stories that provide us with a unique opportunity to preserve our cooking heritage. Yet all of these recipes would mean much less if they didn't have a genuine connection to the heart and soul of our contributors.

As I traveled across the country gathering recipes and preaching about the importance of "passing it down," I met many amazing people who shared their recipes and food stories. In Atlanta, while shopping in a Publix for ingredients for a cooking demonstration at the National Black Arts Festival, I struck up a conversation with an elderly white woman. She was navigating her way with her electric scooter toward the baking section, where our casual conversation rapidly turned to Southern cooking.

We talked about canning peaches and the best way to cook collard greens using scrap meat. She even told me quite emphatically that fried chicken is best if cooked in pork fat. Wow, I thought, that's very interesting. Our cook-to-cook exchange reminded me that Southern whites' cooking was not radically different from Southern blacks' cooking because we helped to define the region's food. While not everything she said was new or something I'd do in my own kitchen, I was really touched that she would so readily pass along such personal advice.

For centuries, it was this kind of sharing that kept African Americans going. On a daily basis, family and friends came together for the main meal of the day and for conversation, and it was in this environment that such kitchen wisdom was exchanged. Growing up in poverty, supper was the one daily event that put a smile on our faces. No matter how poor folks were, supper was often grand. We've lost a lot of traditions, but keeping my family close during Sunday Supper is one ritual that I try to hold on to. There are other, smaller customs that still connect me to my family as well. Just like my grandparents, I've always had an old mayonnaise jar in the freezer filled to the rim with seafood gumbo, or several casserole dishes in the refrigerator. Many dishes I serve today come from my experience as a chef, but the meals served from the Henderson's family table have become the foundation of my cuisine.

How to Use This Book

Filled with poignant memories of the past, and the present triumphs of both the acclaimed and unknown black Americans who impacted the way the whole nation eats, this book also gives voice to everyday people and their triumphs in the kitchen. Through their recipes we sit at their tables and hear their tales of family, friends, their past, and their future.

This volume, like any other traditional cookbook, is arranged according to recipe categories, with like ingredients grouped together; however, its greatest value is in the extras you'll find on every page. Pass It Down Tips & Tricks, time-saving ideas, and healthy alternatives make cooking easier and healthier, while Did You Know? boxes educate and delight. Dishes that are as great for your waistline as they are to eat are marked with a "Heart and Soul" stamp of approval.

The *Pass It Down Cookbook* also explores how African Americans have impacted the economy, the iconography, the preparation, and the very spirit of American foods. Nowhere is this more skillfully reflected than in the contributions of our essayists: In "Presidential Cooks," Adrian Miller explores the impact both enslaved and free Blacks wielded in the White House kitchen; Michael Twitty discovers the depth of his African American food roots through Judaism in "Finding My Way Home"; my co-editor Ramin Ganeshram's "Taking Back the Table" reveals how food and the sting of segregation became a catalyst for her father's activism; Donna Daniels presents a heart-warming story of how her sister expanded her family's worldview through food; Michele Washington's "Ironic Authority" takes on the smiling fictions of Aunt Jemima and Uncle Ben; and Desmonette Hazly discusses the culinary arts as a vehicle for social change in "Sacred Table, Sacred Feast."

We are particularly proud of our Pass It Down Menus that can help readers assemble a casual gathering or a spectacular celebration by pairing recipes from this book. From Easter Sunday Brunch to the Festive Winter Holiday Gathering and the Anytime Ice Cream Social menu, you're certain to find a menu that suits your taste buds to a tee.

Our goal was to create a collection that is both a cookbook and community memoir filled with great food and even better stories. There's something for everyone—even the kids, who will love it when they can cook at your side using Chef Scott Alves Barton's special kid-friendly recipes. The younger generation will also be inspired by the special section featuring up-and-coming chefs. And of course, the book would not be complete without pages where you can record your own recipes and "pass it down" to future generations.

So what's the best way to enjoy the riches of the America I AM *Pass It Down Cookbook?* By looking—and looking again. We're sure that every time you pick it up you'll discover something new in its pages.

We hope, as you read this book, it will become a way to learn about and share the bounty that is the African American contribution, not just to food, but to the very identity of this nation. Turn the pages and join us at the table. After all, our shared experience is the greatest feast of all.

— Jeff Henderson

Introduction

Stirring the Melting Pot:

The African American Imprint on Cooking and Food

BY JOANNE MORRIS

As a member of the creative team behind Tavis Smiley's award-winning America I AM: The African American Imprint exhibit, Joanne Morris wrote select elements and oversaw production of the exhibit's eleven multimedia components and its sound design. Morris has written and produced projects for BET, NBC, Fox, and others. She's also written and produced plays directed by famed filmmaker Charles Burnett.

Sweet candied yams. Savory collard greens. Warm cornbread. Tender ribs lusciously covered in barbeque sauce. Oven-fresh cobbler baked with succulent peaches in a brown sugar nirvana topped with a heavenly crust.

These are just some of the delights of Southern cuisine, known today around the world as *soul food*. While soul food is familiar to many, what is often not recognized is how thoroughly the rich, diverse African American culinary imprint has been stirred into America's melting pot of food. This essential contribution is one of the significant imprints—alongside art, literature, politics, music, and much more—celebrated in the national traveling exhibition, America I AM: The African American Imprint.

On slave barques like the Wildfire, depicted here, foods were used to degrade, cajole, and control African slaves, precious "cargo" though they were.

    With its centuries-old roots grounded in West and Central African cultures and diets, the culinary imprint can still be seen today, whether in choice of ingredients, cooking techniques, or delicious recipes. For instance, both the peanut synonym *goober*[1] and the name of the famed Creole dish *gumbo,*[2] which means "okra," have their origins in the Bantu language family of Central and Southern Africa.[3] And did you know that African barbeque used a flavorful sauce that has become a staple of American grilling cuisine? Or that the old-fashioned version of gingerbread cake derives from a Congolese cake made with dark molasses and ginger-root powder?

Are There Really American Foods of African Descent?

You may be surprised to know which foods were brought to this country through the transatlantic slave trade.[4] Centuries later, we still find some in pantries and on kitchen tables across the country, from sesame seeds and black-eyed peas to peanuts. Originally brought to Africa from Brazil by Portuguese slave traders, the popular peanut was introduced to the colonies through the slave trade. Likewise, yams and watermelons, both specific to African agriculture, traveled across the same ocean route to prosper in Southern soils.

Another food item in American cuisine that benefited from African influence is one we don't readily associate with either Africa or America—rice. In fact, just as cotton and tobacco were cash crops cultivated by enslaved labor, which generated millions of dollars for this nation's colonial and pre–Civil War economies, rice played a major role in the agricultural development of America. Successful rice cultivation was the direct result of the agricultural know-how of enslaved Africans and their American-born descendants.[5] African rice farmers—of which a significant number were women—from areas such as Angola and Senegambia were often targeted by slave traders because of their expertise.[6] Today, rice not only remains an American food staple, but the United States is the fourth largest exporter of rice in the world.[7]

Clearly, the hands-on role of enslaved African Americans in planting, growing, and harvesting food, particularly in the South, helped to define the emerging American cuisine. But the imprint would be greatest in how these foods were prepared.

Did the Collision of Cultures Impact the Imprint?

Though enslaved Africans were living in the Spanish colony of St. Augustine, Florida in the late 1500s, the virtual seeds of the African American culinary imprint were planted in August 1619 with the arrival of the 20 African men and women in England's first permanent colony in Jamestown, Virginia.[8] Over the centuries, the African American population would grow into thousands and then millions.[9] Among them were West and Central Africans from hundreds of culturally diverse tribes, who spoke just as many languages.

It was the collision of cultures—West and Central African, European, and Native American populations—that created the foundation of American culture and cuisine. However, with enslaved blacks outnumbering the white population in many places, the African American food imprint often dominated because, as Jessica B. Harris has noted, they "planted it, grew it, harvested it, cooked it, served it . . ." (*Iron Pots & Wooden Spoons: Africa's Gifts to New World Cooking*).

Although Africans who were captured and sold into slavery could not bring their possessions to America, they brought their cultural memories, which included how they prepared foods. These cooking techniques were used both in the slaveholder's kitchen and in the slave quarters where they cooked for their own families.[10]

One of these techniques was deep-frying—with peanut oil or lard—which, over time, became a standard method in American cooking.[11] In fact, this African practice led to the elevation of a staple food of African descent to an American classic—fried chicken. Enslaved Africans applied several cooking methods to create dishes that are American favorites to this day. For example, they adapted how they made *eba*[12] to hominy, turning it into glorious grits, and how they baked *fufu*[13] is the same way they made cornbread.

As noted earlier, barbeque sauce is another African culinary import. Africans had their own style of barbeque that incorporated a sauce made of chili and sweet peppers. The Timucua Indians of Florida were recorded cooking meat using the *barbacoa* method by European colonizers as early as the 1560s. These influences would combine to form this unique Southern style of cooking.

The influence of African culture on the American palate is well documented in both history books and cookbooks. From the shores of West Africa to the plantation kitchens of the American South, the foods and ingredients they used are entwined in American cuisine and can now be found on the menus of restaurants around the country.

The African American Food Imprint in the North

Once in America, the people stolen from West and Central Africa represented the breadth of social backgrounds—from aristocrats to artisans, farmers to soldiers.[14] They were sold throughout the Southern and Northern colonies alike until the early 1800s. Slaves in Northern urban areas were often not confined to service

An elderly African American couple has a solemn meal
in their tidy rural Virginia home in 1864, during the Civil War.

in the master's house. These workers would often be sent to sell food on the street, making extra money for their slaveholder.[15] It was enslaved street vendors who took their home cooking, influenced by their African heritage, into the streets of America's growing cities.

Many Northern states had pre-Emancipation communities of free African Americans. Massachusetts, for example, had abolished slavery by 1783,[16] and New York fully in 1827.[17] While these free blacks had business owners, lawyers, teachers, and ministers among them, there were still many who were hired as housekeepers and cooks.[18] It was these African Americans in the North, including those who escaped captivity, who would also help solidify the national imprint of African American cooking methods. And as more black Southerners moved North during and after the Civil War, and again as part of the early 20th-century Great

Migration, dishes that were once considered solely the domain of the South became as commonplace in Chicago as they were in Charleston.

As African Americans populated states outside the South, their soulful recipes from back home were passed down from generation to generation. Whether through storytelling or handwritten recipes, these heirlooms included everything from secret cooking ingredients to special ways of kneading dough for monkey bread.[19] These culinary inheritances allowed Southern cuisine to become a living tradition across the country.

What If There Were No African American Imprint on Food?

It's hard to imagine this nation without the African American culinary imprint. There would be no more eating grandma's signature fried chicken at Sunday dinners. No more steaming plates of chitterlings and black-eyed peas on New Year's Day. No more family reunions with passionate contests between relatives to see who created the spiciest or most savory barbequed ribs. No more getting your soul filled with soul food.

Stirring the Melting Pot

Foods made by African Americans with African cooking methods and transplanted African foods have existed for centuries in America, yet the use of the term "soul food" to describe African-inspired Southern dishes did not occur until the 1960s. But whether you call it soul food or Southern cooking, this food imprint is an integral part of American cuisine.

As a result, the African American food imprint continues to inspire America's imagination and please taste buds. From Thanksgiving Day platters of candied yams on dining tables across the country to the availability of canned collard greens and packaged cornbread at the supermarket, from barbeque joints in Manhattan and Seattle to Southern-born fried chicken franchises in cities and towns across America, the gastronomic descendents of those foods and recipes introduced by enslaved Africans are welcomed in every home and in every state. The African American culinary imprint has become an indelible part of American cuisine that continues to stir our melting pot and nourish the heart and soul of this nation every day.

Then as now, Sunday was a day not just to worship but to gather, socialize, and spend a little time relaxing that often lasted the whole day and into the evening. Talented cooks, both male and female, lent their hands to feeding crowds either by potluck or marathon cooking sessions in the church or meeting house kitchen. One-pot dishes, like Brunswick stew, burgoo, jambalaya, or gumbo that could feed a crowd for little money always had a place at the table.

CHAPTER **1**

Starters, Soups & Salads

Nicole Taylor's Backyard Pecans with Rosemary

Brooklyn, New York

SERVES 4 TO 6

Source: Jordan A. Colbert

Atlanta-raised Nicole Taylor is the host of Hot Grease *on the Heritage Food Radio Network. These aromatically spiced pecans were born from her fond memories of picking pecans in her family's Georgia backyard as well as Thanksgiving and Christmas parties that remind her of "passing the nutcracker and pecans around the room." They are, says Ms. Taylor, her favorite pre-meal nibble or anytime snack.*

2 cups Georgia pecans
1 teaspoon (heaping) coarse salt
½ teaspoon cinnamon
4 tablespoons unsalted butter
¼ cup dark brown sugar
1 tablespoon chopped fresh rosemary

Pass It Down TIP

This spicy, sweet snack is a perfect carry-along for your lunch bag.

Toss pecans in large skillet over low-medium heat. Toast around 10 minutes. Set aside in small mixing bowl.

Combine cinnamon and salt. Set aside.

Melt butter in skillet over low-medium heat. Add sugar and rosemary, stir until golden brown. Add pecans to the skillet and coat well.

Transfer to small mixing bowl. Sprinkle with salt mixture and toss. Place in festive bowl and provide cocktail napkins.

Justin Gilette's Low-Country Crab Cakes

Atlanta, Georgia

SERVES 4 TO 6

Source: Jihad Ziyad

Justin Gillette's knack for cooking began after a baseball injury forced him to choose a different elective course in 10th grade. He chose a culinary class. Today, Gillette, a 26-year-old self-professed foodie who works full time as a chef for the food service company Sodexho, is intrigued by every facet of the culinary world. He has traveled internationally, soaking in the culture and cuisine of Portugal and Spain, from Madrid, Seville, and Segovia to the southern tip of the Costa del Sol, to Morocco in North Africa, and Alaska. His style of cooking can be described as the low country type, but similar to New Orleans cuisine. It's flavorful and robust, much like food cooked in Charleston and Savannah, but with a spin of French and Spanish cuisine around the edges.

2 tablespoons butter
¼ cup small onion, chopped
2 teaspoons fresh thyme
¼ cup diced celery stalk
1 teaspoon salt
2 teaspoons ground black pepper
1 cup mayonnaise
2 tablespoons Dijon mustard
4 shakes of Tabasco sauce
1 teaspoon celery seed
½ teaspoon cayenne pepper
3 teaspoons sugar
2 large eggs
1 pound lump crab meat
1 cup bread crumbs
2 cloves garlic, chopped

Pass It Down TIP

Crab cakes freeze easily and can keep up to six months when stored properly. Double or triple this recipe and freeze the extra cakes for a last minute party, brunch, or special appetizer. Simply form the raw crab cakes and place them in a single layer on wax paper inside a freezer-safe, sealable container. Place another sheet of wax paper on top of the crab cakes and add another layer of crab cakes on top. Seal tightly and freeze. To use: Remove crab cakes as needed and defrost in the refrigerator in a sealed container. Once defrosted, cook crab cakes as you normally would.

In a hot skillet, melt 1 tablespoon of the butter. Add the onions, garlic, thyme, and celery. Sauté until the mixture becomes translucent. Set aside to cool.

In a bowl, mix the mayonnaise, mustard, Tabasco, celery seed, cayenne pepper, sugar, and egg. Mix until thoroughly combined.

Add the cooled onion mixture to the bowl and mix well. Gently fold in the crab meat. When completely mixed, add the bread crumbs to bind the mixture together, adding more as needed to achieve a moldable consistency.

Form the crab meat mixture into small patties, about 3–4 inches in diameter. Place on a tray lined with parchment. Chill in the refrigerator, covered in plastic wrap, for at least 1 hour and up to 8 hours.

Heat the remaining tablespoon of the butter in a skillet on medium-high heat. When melted, place the crab cakes in the pan and cook on each side until golden brown—about 5–8 minutes. Serve with Remoulade Sauce (page 231).

Mrs. Robinson's Spinach & Cheese Quiche

Richmond Heights, Ohio

SERVES 4 TO 6

Source: LaToya Jackson

Carol Robinson's spinach and cheese quiche is her family's traditional brunch, special breakfast dish, or even a snack. The quiche is the object of desire of numerous friends and family members who, she says, are always asking for the recipe. "This is an easy, delicious, aroma-smelling quiche that will make your taste buds come to life," she says. *"My husband says it's one of the best things I have ever made for him."*

½ teaspoon salt
½ teaspoon pepper
5 ounces shredded Swiss cheese
3 ounces shredded Parmesan cheese
1 9-inch deep-dish frozen piecrust
1 tablespoon canola oil
⅓ cup chopped onions
1 tablespoon minced garlic
5 ounces fresh spinach, chopped or
    frozen chopped spinach, thawed
5 eggs, lightly beaten
1 cup half-and-half

Pass It Down TIP

Carol Robinson suggests cutting the quiche in slices and storing in plastic wrap in the freezer. The quiche can be reheated easily or popped frozen into the microwave for a quick snack or easy lunch.

Preheat oven to 350° F.

In a medium bowl, mix the salt, pepper, and both cheeses. Place this mixture in the frozen piecrust.

Heat the oil in a skillet over medium heat, and cook the onions until tender. Mix in the garlic and spinach. Cook until the spinach has wilted or until the liquid has evaporated, if using frozen.

Remove the skillet from heat and pour the mixture into the pie shell over the cheeses.

Mix the eggs and half-and-half in a bowl and pour the egg mixture over the top of spinach mixture in the pie shell. Top the mixture with additional cheese if desired.

Bake in the preheated oven for 45 minutes or until top of quiche begins to turn lightly brown.

Mum's Ham Bone Soup Bajan Style

Boston, Massachusetts

SERVES 6 TO 8

Leslie Forde is vice president of international strategy and partnerships at the social networking company Communispace. A professionally trained chef, she primarily credits her mother with teaching her to cook through observation. After college, experimentation and voracious cookbook reading led to a turn at Le Cordon Bleu, where she earned a pastry degree, but her culinary hero remained her mother and her home-style cooking from her native Barbados. "My mum is an amazing natural cook who can whip up a feast fit for kings from whatever is on hand. Many of her dishes are influenced by our Bajan heritage. This soup never disappoints and can be made with just about any veggies that you happen to have on hand. It's also wonderful with chicken or turkey, but the ham bone creates this lovely, complex flavor."

SOUP

1 ham bone with a generous amount of ham still on it
2 large onions, chopped
1½ cups homemade chicken stock (p. 13)
1 cup green split peas
1–2 sweet potatoes, cut into large cubes
3 russet potatoes, cut into large cubes
1 large carrot, sliced into ¼-inch rounds
1 ancho chili or other hot red pepper
1 spring onion, chopped
5 thyme sprigs
1 bay leaf
hot pepper sauce (from Barbados) or other aromatic hot sauce to taste
seasoning salt and fresh ground black pepper to taste

DUMPLINGS

1 cup flour
2 tablespoons sugar
1 teaspoon allspice
1 teaspoon salt
¼ cup cold water or more, as needed

Put the ham bone and 2 chopped onions into a large (8-quart) stockpot. Fill to two inches from the top with cold water. Bring to boil on high heat and reduce to simmer for 1 hour.

Add the chicken stock, reduce heat to medium high, and add the sweet potatoes, russet potatoes, carrot, ancho chili, spring onion, thyme sprigs, and bay leaf. Simmer until the vegetables are tender, about 1½ hours.

Make the dumplings while the vegetables are cooking: Combine the flour, sugar, allspice, and salt in a bowl. Whisk until all ingredients are combined. Add the water to the flour mixture until it comes together in a sticky dough. Form the dough into two-inch balls, then flatten each ball with your palm. Add the dumplings to soup about 45 minutes to an hour after the vegetables have been added. Cook 45 minutes more.

Spice finished soup with pepper sauce, salt, and black pepper to taste.

··· Three Basic Stock Recipes ···

Stocks are not simply the start of delicious soups. They can add depth to stews, are the basis of sauces, and are ideal for flavorfully boiling grains such as rice. Adding flavor through stock means you can cut down on butter, fats, and salt to give these foods added taste. And speaking of salt, you'll notice that none of these stock recipes have any. The boiling-down process would intensify the salty taste, making the stock less versatile as a basis for other dishes. Salt stock only if you don't intend to use it in a recipe that requires further reduction.

Vegetable Stock

MAKES ABOUT 8 QUARTS

Virtually any vegetable can be used in vegetable stock, although certain ones, like cauliflower, cabbage, broccoli, and others in that family, are considered overpowering in flavor and are best avoided. Tomato in small quantity can add color and taste, but can make the stock more like tomato broth if too much is used.

4 pounds assorted vegetables, or well-washed vegetable trimmings
1 large onion, chopped roughly
10 sprigs thyme
1 teaspoon peppercorns
2 bay leaves
2 cloves garlic

Place all ingredients in a 12-quart (or larger) stock pot.

Add 2 gallons (32 cups) of cold water.

Bring ingredients to a simmer, skimming any accumulated scum from the surface as needed.

Simmer for 1 hour, strain, and cool completely. Refrigerate for up to 5 days.

Beef Stock

MAKES ABOUT 6 QUARTS

This recipe can be used for venison, bison, and most other game or livestock—except pork. Roasting the bones prior to throwing them into the stockpot adds rich flavor, although it is not strictly necessary.

10 pounds raw beef bones and meaty trimmings
2 medium carrots, peeled and cut into 2-inch pieces
2 celery stalks, cut into 2-inch pieces
1 large yellow onion, peeled and quartered
5 cloves garlic, peeled
1 tablespoon whole black peppercorns
1 small bunch parsley, with stems, washed well
4 sprigs thyme

(Optional) Place bones and trimmings in a broiler pan. Broil in the oven broiler until caramelized, about 25 minutes.

Place the bones, carrots, celery, onion, garlic, and peppercorns in a 12-quart (or larger) stockpot.

Add 2 gallons (32 cups) cold water.

Tie parsley and thyme together with a piece of kitchen twine and add to the pot. Bring ingredients to a simmer, skimming any accumulated scum from the surface as needed.

Simmer for 4 hours, strain, and cool completely. Use immediately for soups or sauce, or refrigerate for up to 5 days.

Chicken Stock

As with beef stock, chicken stock benefits from roasting the bones and trimming prior to boiling.

10 pounds raw chicken or turkey bones with meaty trimmings
2 medium carrots, peeled and cut into 2-inch pieces
2 celery stalks, cut into 2-inch pieces
1 large yellow onion, peeled and quartered
5 cloves garlic, peeled
1 tablespoon whole black peppercorns
1 small bunch parsley, with stems, washed well
4 sprigs thyme

(Optional) Place bones and trimmings in a broiler pan and broil in the oven broiler until caramelized, about 25 minutes.

Place the bones, carrots, celery, onion, garlic, and peppercorns in a 12-quart (or larger) stockpot.

Add 2 gallons (32 cups) cold water.

Tie the parsley and thyme together with a piece of kitchen twine and add that to the pot. Bring ingredients to a simmer, skimming any accumulated scum from the surface as needed.

Simmer for 4 hours, strain, and cool completely. Use immediately for soup or sauce, or refrigerate for up to 5 days.

Pass It Down trick: *Freeze stocks in 1 to 2 cup portions in freezer-safe containers for later use. Mark the date on the container and don't use stock older than 1–2 months.*

Store vegetable, meat, and bone trimmings in freezer-safe baggies, with dates clearly marked, to use for making stock.

Chef Jeff's Collard Green Soup with Smoked Turkey

Las Vegas, Nevada
SERVES 6 TO 8

There are many ways to cook greens. Some great home cooks use three types: collards, mustards, and turnips. Chef Jeff took the collared green recipe from his big sister, turned it into a soup, and then put a healthy spin on it. "I once served this soup at a National Heart Association conference. The participants still write to me to tell me how much they loved the recipe.

8 cups of fat-free, low-sodium chicken broth or homemade stock (see recipe page 13)
1 tablespoon garlic powder
1 small smoked turkey drumstick
1 medium yellow onion, diced small
1 bunch of organic collared greens, stems removed and roughly chopped
5 cups purified water
salt or salt alternative to taste
freshly ground white pepper to taste

In a stockpot over medium heat, add chicken broth, garlic powder, and turkey drumstick.

Sauté onion until translucent—don't let it burn—then add onions and greens to stockpot and pour in the water. Reduce heat to a simmer. Cook for 1 hour or until greens are tender.

Remove turkey from pot. Let turkey cool and then remove meat from bone. Roughly chop meat and set aside. Season with salt (or salt alternate) and white pepper to taste.

Remove greens from broth and set aside. Strain broth and put back into the pot.

Season with salt or salt alternative and pepper to taste.

Pour broth into bowls. Add turkey and greens.

Pass It Down TIP

This is a delicious soup to serve year-round. Turkey is used as a healthy alternative meat for this recipe. It adds great flavor to the soup.

··· Finding My Way Home ···

BY MICHAEL TWITTY

Source: Michael Twitty

Michael Twitty is a native of Washington, DC who learned to cook from watching his grandmother and from the patient teaching of his mother. Today he is a recognized food historian who takes recipes from the past and uses heirloom, organic, and heritage-breed ingredients to re-create historic and traditional dishes that are part of what he calls "our own edible jazz." Twitty was instrumental in helping the D. Landreth Seed Company, which has been in business since 1784, develop a catalog of African American heritage seeds released in 2009. He is the creator of www.afrofoodways. com, the first Web site devoted to the preservation of historic African American foods and foodways.

At age seven, I read Chaim Potok's book *The Chosen*, the story of the binding friendship between two Jewish boys in Brooklyn, New York in 1940. I was utterly fascinated—an exploration my mother indulged by allowing me to "be Jewish" for a week, which ultimately amounted to me not eating any pork. But the book and the strong tie to religious culture stayed with me, and in 2002, at age 25, I converted to Judaism.

When I became Jewish, my whole worldview as an African American and my take on African American culture changed. I thought I couldn't have any more respect or love for my roots, any deeper sense of pride—and converting to Judaism, in my case, changed that. Far from removing me from my heritage, it brought me closer to the stories and lives of our ancestors.

Here I was, confronted with a religious culture that used food repeatedly as an edible textbook—to transmit history, ethics, culture, geography, customs, and family traditions. The Passover Seder is all about using food to tell the story of slavery and redemption from slavery. That sent me back into the world into which I was born looking for the culinary genealogy that was my birthright. I had to teach the Holocaust in Hebrew school, and I wanted to soften the lesson with something more palatable, so I chose a book called *In Memory's Kitchen* by Cara De Silva. She wrote about the women of Terezin, Hitler's "model" ghetto/concentration camp, and how they recalled their prize heirloom recipes even in the midst of hell.

It hit me: What if enslaved Africans—the oldest cooks in human history—and their descendants could have such a record, told in food, of their struggle to survive, persevere, overcome, and be free? That's what set me on my journey.

Tracing the roots of our food from West and Central Africa to the present day through enslavement has not been easy. I have forced myself into the cotton, rice, tobacco, and cornfields to experience a taste of the brutality that made our cuisine in chains so precious at the end of those "can to can't" working days. It's not easy putting on the garb of an enslaved person and cooking in the same kitchens that fed the families of the planters or in the few remaining slave cabins that dot the landscape.

But when I remember I'm doing honor to the forgotten chefs who invented Southern cooking, it sweetens the experience. I want African Americans as a people to embrace our heirloom produce, our traditional foods, and the recipes that can and will be lost if we don't reclaim them and own them as part of our legacy. Jewish tradition tells you to "Bless the Lord and eat and be satisfied." African American tradition bids us to "sit at the welcome table." By weaving those traditions together I've found my way "home."

> "It's not easy putting on the garb of an enslaved person and cooking in the same kitchens that fed the families of the planters or in the few remaining slave cabins that dot the landscape; but when I remember I'm doing honor to the forgotten chefs who invented Southern cooking, it sweetens the experience."

Michael Twitty's Heirloom Cowhorn Okra Soup

Baltimore, Maryland

SERVES 4 TO 6

"Cowhorn Okra Soup is just one example of the music of soul food," writes Michael Twitty. "From Senegal to Angola, from Jamaica to Haiti, and later from Baltimore to Savannah to New Orleans, one traditional soup stands out as a reminder of the undying connection to West and Central Africa. Known as supakanja (kanja or kanjo means 'okra' among the West Atlantic speakers of Senegambia and Sierra Leone) in West Africa, okra has many names along the coast from which our ancestors came. This recipe was popular on both the table of the plantation owner and his enslaved workforce along the entire southeastern seaboard and Gulf coast. Cowhorn okra, a crisp heirloom variety is rooted from okra seed brought to America during the slave trade. This recipe is over 250 years old."

2 medium yellow onions, sliced or chopped
3 tablespoons flour
2 or 3 tablespoons bacon drippings, lard, vegetable oil, or butter
2½ quarts of water
1 dried or salted fish that's been soaked overnight **or**
1 cup salt pork or bacon pieces or smoked turkey (see vegetarian option below)
3 cups tomatoes, chopped
2 pounds okra, sliced
1 long red cayenne pepper or Maryland Fish pepper, sliced in half
herbs of your choice (bits of parsley, rosemary, basil, etc.)
salt to taste
1 cup cooked crabmeat (optional)

Heat the oil or drippings until hot but not smoking.

Dust the onions in the flour. Add them to the pot with the heated oil and sauté until translucent. Add the water and choice of meat and cook for 2½ hours. This creates the stock for the soup.

Add the remaining ingredients and simmer another 2 hours.

Pass It Down TIP

You can make this dish using fresh chicken to replace the other meats. Simply lightly brown the chicken with the frying onions, then add enough water to cover it by 1 inch. Simmer for 2½ hours. To make this a vegetarian dish, ignore the meats and replace the water with vegetable stock, preferably organic.

Apryle's Seafood Gumbo

Charlotte, North Carolina

SERVES 10

Rhonda Dorsey-Prude is an Army veteran who says that, while she loved good food, she was never that good in the kitchen. But time and practice changed all that—along with a few must-have recipes gained from friends and family, like this one from her sister Apryle. It forgoes both roux and the holy trinity of Louisiana gumbo—pepper, onion, and celery, proving what a versatile and adaptable dish gumbo is. Ms. Dorsey-Prude remembers the first day she had Apryle's seafood gumbo back in 1987 and how intent folks were on getting every last delicious drop from their bowls. "The table was so quiet it was crazy," she says. "You heard spoons hitting against the porcelain."

3½ cups plain tomato sauce
10½ cups of water
1 teaspoon gumbo filé (powdered sassafras leaf)
2 teaspoons Old Bay Seasoning to taste
1 pound andouille sausage, sliced into ½-inch rounds
1 pound medium sea scallops
1 pound lump crab meat
1 pound fresh oysters
4 ears corn, halved
2 pounds medium shrimp, shelled and deveined
6–8 okra, chopped

Bring tomato sauce and water to a boil in a large stockpot with the gumbo filé. Add the Old Bay Seasoning to taste.

Simmer 45 minutes. Add the andouille sausage and all seafood except the shrimp. Remove the ends of the okra, dice them, and add them to the pot. Continue to simmer for another hour.

Add the corn in the last 20 minutes of cooking, and add the shrimp in the last 15 minutes of cooking. Turn off the heat and allow the gumbo to sit 20 minutes before serving, stirring every 5 minutes.

Serve over white rice.

Did you know? *Gumbo filé is powdered sassafras leaves and was used for both medicine and as seasoning for soups and stews among Native Americans.*

Eric Spigner's Everything in the Pot Gumbo

Dallas, Texas

SERVES 20

Source: Eric T. Springer

Eric Spigner, a professional chef who owns his own catering business in Texas, was originally taught at home in South Carolina at "Grandma's" cooking school. He says the inspiration behind this recipe was his son's first birthday party. Wanting to create something that would bring all the guests together "while blowing their culinary minds," he decided to kick up a Southern classic with a wider variety of meats and vegetables. Thai sriracha sauce, rather than Tabasco, adds a spicy new twist to this dish, which is so ample that it's ideal for a large party, family gathering, or church supper.

¾ cup canola oil
3 large Vidalia or other sweet onions, roughly chopped
3 large green bell peppers, stemmed, seeded, and thinly sliced
3 large red bell peppers, stemmed, seeded, and thinly sliced
12 scallions, trimmed and finely chopped
12 garlic cloves, crushed
2 jalapeño peppers, minced
1 boneless chicken breast chopped into 1-inch chunks
1 smoked beef sausage chopped into 1-inch chunks
1 cup flour
8 cups water
4 cups seafood stock or fish stock
1 large bag frozen cut okra
1 large bag frozen sweet corn
1 tablespoon freshly ground black pepper
3 teaspoons sriracha pepper sauce (available in Asian markets)
4 teaspoons ground cumin
3 teaspoons turmeric
3 teaspoons coriander
2 pounds crawfish meat

Pass It Down TIP

An incredibly simple seafood stock is easy to make quickly and on an as-needed basis. Simply toss 1 cup of shellfish tails, heads, and shells into 6 cups of water and simmer for 30 minutes, or until the stock is reduced by one-third. Use or freeze for later use.

6 ounces catfish, filleted and chopped in 1-inch chunks
1 pound medium shrimp, tailed, peeled, and deveined
2 tablespoons kosher salt (or more to taste)

Heat ¼ cup of canola oil in a large fry pan and add the onions and red and green bell peppers. Fry on low-medium heat until the onions are translucent and peppers are softened. Add the scallions, garlic, and jalapeño peppers and fry for 2–3 minutes more or until garlic just begins to brown. Add the chicken breast and beef sausage, and fry until the chicken breast is lightly browned. Remove from heat and set aside.

Heat the remaining oil in a large, deep stockpot and add the flour. Cook over low-medium heat, stirring constantly until you achieve a dark paste (roux) the color of molasses.

In another saucepan, heat the water and stock to a simmer. Add the water and stock to the roux and mix, using a whisk until totally dissolved and combined.

Add the pepper and onion mixture to the pot with the roux mixture and add the okra, corn, black pepper, sriracha pepper sauce, cumin, turmeric, and coriander. Mix well. Simmer for 30 minutes.

Add the crawfish, catfish, and shrimp. Simmer 20 minutes more. Mix in the salt and simmer 10 minutes more.

Serve over white rice.

• •

Did you know? *Sriracha is a Thai pepper sauce made from chilies, vinegar, salt, and sugar. While it is most often found in Asian and Middle Eastern markets, more and more regular supermarkets sell sriracha sauce in the Asian food aisle. But be careful, it packs one spicy punch!*

• •

Leslie Forde's Grilled Shrimp Salad with Veggies

Boston, Massachusetts

SERVES 4 AS A STARTER, 2 AS A MAIN DISH

This is a light, fresh recipe that is big on taste thanks to freshly grilled veggies and a sweet and sour vinaigrette. The recipe can be a nice starter salad for a summer meal or a meal in itself for two. Showing her Caribbean roots, Leslie Forde says she prefers wild-caught versus farm-raised shrimp for this dish because of their fresher, sweeter flavor.

SALAD

10 large or jumbo-size shrimp, peeled, and deveined
2 tablespoons lemon zest
juice from ½ lemon
2 large garlic cloves, chopped
3 tablespoons fresh rosemary, chopped
½ pound baby yams or sweet potatoes, sliced thinly
6 large white mushrooms, cleaned with stems removed
1 Scotch bonnet (or another spicy pepper, like a habañero)
¼ cup extra virgin olive oil
2 tablespoons balsamic vinegar
salt and fresh ground pepper to taste
2 cups baby spinach (rinsed and dried if not already prewashed)
1 cup grape tomatoes, sliced into halves

VINAIGRETTE

⅓ cup extra virgin olive oil
1 tablespoon sherry vinegar
1 teaspoon honey
salt and pepper to taste

Pass It Down TIP

Clean mushrooms without waterlogging them by wiping them gently with a paper towel immediately after washing.

Marinate the shrimp: Rinse shrimp in cold water and place in a small bowl with the lemon zest, juice, garlic, and rosemary. Stir lightly to combine. Cover with plastic wrap and refrigerate for at least 1 hour and up to 4.

While the shrimp is marinating, prepare vegetables for the grill by placing them into a bowl and adding the olive oil. Toss well to coat and add the balsamic vinegar, salt, and fresh ground pepper to taste. Stir well and set aside.

Heat grill to about 500° F.

Place marinated vegetables on the grill and cook until the potato slices are soft and turn a lighter orange color, about 4 or 5 minutes per side. Remove from grill and set aside.

Grill mushrooms until they're dark and soft, about 4 minutes. Remove from heat and set aside.

Grill Scotch bonnet pepper, turning often, until there are grill marks on all sides. Remove from heat and set aside. When cool, remove stem and seeds and slice thinly. Set aside.

Place marinated shrimp onto the top rack of the grill or away from direct heat, if the grill has only one level. Grill on each side until the shrimp is pink, about 1 to 2 minutes per side.

Divide the spinach and tomatoes into two or four salad bowls, depending on whether it's an appetizer or main dish. Divide the grilled vegetables between the bowls, arranging them evenly over the spinach and tomatoes.

Top each salad with 5 grilled shrimp for two, or 2–3 for serving four.

Whisk all the sherry vinaigrette ingredients together and pour over each salad. Serve immediately.

· ·

Pass It Down trick: *The "gills," or the brown flesh on the underside of the cap, absorb a great deal of oil, which is not only less than healthful but can prevent even browning or grilling. For larger mushrooms with gills, like portabellos, gently scrape away the gills from the underside of the cap using a small teaspoon. Reserve the trimmed gills for vegetable stock.*

· ·

Ron Duprat's Jicama Slaw

Naples, Florida

SERVES 4 TO 6 AS A SIDE DISH

Heart & Soul

Source: Tameka Crout

Haitian-born chef Ron Duprat rose to fame after a Season Six stint on Bravo's Top Chef. *Mr. Duprat has known poverty, near-starvation, and a harrowing 27-day passage as a teenager in an open-hull boat with little water and even less food in the company of 250 others fleeing his native Haiti. The chef says that some of his earliest memories are of working alongside his grandmother in Haiti, cooking the fish they caught to survive and gathering fresh produce from his father's garden. "The unique tastes, smells, and feelings created alongside my grandmother are things that cannot be taught in a sterile classroom but are learned by immersion. It comes with the territory, as food is not only designed to nourish us, but serve as life-long memories," says Chef Duprat, who nourishes a larger culinary goal: "to bring people together in my personal cause to fight childhood hunger, especially in Africa and Haiti." His slaw recipe uses crunchy Caribbean jicama and plain yogurt for a refreshing side to traditional fried chicken, barbecue, and roasted meats and vegetables.*

1 cup plain yogurt
3 tablespoons lime juice
2 tablespoons cider vinegar
2 tablespoons sugar
1 tablespoon chopped cilantro leaves
1 teaspoon ground cumin
1 teaspoon salt
½ teaspoon freshly ground black pepper
3 cups shredded or julienned jicama
½ bunch green onions, sliced thinly on the bias
1 red bell pepper, thinly sliced

Whisk together the yogurt, lime juice, cider vinegar, sugar, cilantro, cumin, salt, and pepper. Refrigerate for at least 30 minutes to allow flavors to mingle.

When ready to serve, combine the jicama, green onions, and red bell pepper in a large bowl and add the dressing. Toss gently but thoroughly to combine. Season with additional salt and pepper, to taste.

Mom's Deviled Eggs

Springfield, Ohio

SERVES 6

Virginia Jones,
Debra Wilkerson's mother

Source: Debra Wilkerson

The exact history of deviling eggs is unknown, but the idea of liberally spicing—or "deviling"—eggs goes back a few thousand years. One of the staple foods in the South, deviled eggs were most popular in the summertime, when laying hens were turning out eggs faster than most folks could cook, sell, or give them away. Scooping out the yolks and mixing them with simple seasonings like salt, pepper, mayonnaise, and mustard was and is the norm but folks will put just about anything in these bite-sized beauties, from relish to anchovies, caviar to chilies, shrimp to chives and more. However you eat them, deviled eggs are a star attraction at picnics and potlucks and Debra Wilkerson's mom's recipe for classic "sweet and sour" deviled eggs is a must-have favorite at family events.

12 hard-boiled eggs, peeled and sliced in half
1 tablespoon sugar
3 tablespoons cider vinegar
⅓ cup Miracle Whip or mayonnaise
salt and pepper to taste
paprika for garnish

Slice each egg in half lengthwise. Using a small teaspoon, gently remove egg yolks from the egg whites.

Place the yolks in a bowl and mash with a fork until crumbly.

Add the sugar, cider vinegar, Miracle Whip or mayonnaise, salt and pepper. Mix well until creamy and, using the spoon, gently refill each egg white with an equal amount of yolk mixture.

Sprinkle with paprika. Chill, covered, for up to 3 hours.

Pass It Down healthy variation: *Substitute low-fat sour cream or non-fat strained yogurt for the Miracle Whip or mayonnaise. Alternatively, use hummus in place of the egg yolk to stuff the egg whites.*

Soul Food Museum Southern Style Potato Salad

Atlanta, Georgia

SERVES 10 TO 12

As the owner of The Soul Food Museum, the only museum in the world celebrating African American's contributions to the culinary arts and hospitality, Dr. Kenneth Willhoite has a long index of recipes for great-tasting dishes for every type of event. He says his Soul Food Museum Southern Style Potato Salad is great to eat year round, but is a must-have for Juneteenth, family reunions, and of course, barbeques.

5 pounds Idaho potatoes
1 dozen eggs
½ cup mustard
1 tablespoon apple cider vinegar
1 tablespoon sugar
1 cup mayonnaise
1 large onion, diced very small
3 stalks of celery, diced very small
1 medium jar of sweet pickle relish
1–2 tablespoons paprika
2 tablespoons fresh parsley
Salt and pepper to taste

Pass It Down TIP

The perfect hard-boiled egg is not so much boiled as steeped in hot water. First, bring eggs to room temperature so they don't crack when they are heated up. Place your eggs in the bottom of a pot in one layer and don't stack them on top of each other. Add enough cold water to cover the eggs by about 1 inch of water. Place the pot on medium-high heat. Once the water is boiling rapidly, remove the pot from the heat and cover tightly with the lid. Let the eggs sit for 17 minutes (large eggs) or 20 minutes (jumbo eggs). Pour off the cooking water and place the eggs in cold water to cool down. Peel and use.

Cook potatoes until the skin is tender when stuck with a fork then remove skin and mash.

Boil eggs and cut into small pieces. Set aside pieces from three of the eggs for garnish. Mix the potatoes and eggs then add in the mustard, apple cider vinegar, sugar, mayonnaise, onion, celery, and relish. Add salt and pepper to taste. Additional mustard and mayonnaise cab be added for a moister texture. Chill overnight to bring out the best flavor.

Garnish with paprika, fresh parsley, and sliced eggs. Serve warm or chilled.

CK's Brie in Puffed Pastry

New York, New York

SERVES 4

Source: Chaz Kyser

Chaz Foster-Kyser is a fan of easy-to-make meals, and loves that this scrumptious pastry takes only 10 minutes to prepare yet smells, tastes, and looks delicious. The recipe was passed down to her from Dr. Derina Holtzhausen, one of her former professors, who prepared it for an end-of-semester student get-together. "She served it as an appetizer, but I ate so much of it that I didn't have any room for dinner," Foster-Kyser says. "It's great for small parties and is sure to impress your guests."

1 puff pastry sheet (package comes with 2 sheets)
1 tablespoon butter
¼ cup walnuts, chopped
1 egg, beaten
1 small wheel of Brie (8 ounces)
½ cup raspberry or strawberry preserves

This dish's sweet taste makes it perfect for dessert.

Preheat oven to 375° F.

Defrost 1 sheet of puff pastry and unfold. Place the remaining sheet back in the freezer for later use.

Melt butter in a sauce pan over medium-low heat. Add the nuts and sauté until golden brown, about 2–3 minutes. Remove from heat and set aside to cool.

Brush the side of the pastry sheet facing you with the beaten egg.

Scrape the rind off of the Brie with a butter knife, and then center the wheel of Brie on top of the pastry sheet. Gently spread the jam on top of the Brie and then the nuts on top of the jam. Bring all four corners of the sheet together above the Brie and fold them across each other so they overlap. Brush the top and sides of the pastry sheet with the beaten egg. You can be creative and use bits of the other puff pastry sheet to make a bow or other design for the top of the brie.

Place your little masterpiece on an ungreased cookie sheet. Bake for 20–25 minutes or until the pastry is golden brown.

Serve with top-quality wheat crackers such as Pepperidge Farm's Harvest Wheat Crackers.

··· Passing It Down Online à Deux ···

BY CHRYSTAL BAKER

Source: Chrystal Baker

Chrystal Baker and Amir Thomas are young Los Angeleans whose blog Duo Dishes is an exploration of the soul food and home cooking they've grown up with—with new millennium twists. The blog also features the pair trying their hands at everything from cheese grits fries to Vietnamese, Persian, and other international cuisines. A perfect product of African American heritage and 21st-century techno-savvy, the Duo Dishes are just one example of the soulful future of passing our foodways down.

The Duo Dishes, Chrystal Baker and Amir Thomas, are a Los Angeles-based food blogging pair who mix up old school recipes and new school styling for 21st-century African American culinary flair.

We enjoy new tastes, textures, and creations, but we also love the simpler foods from our pasts. Adding a modern spin on the traditional is inspiring and enriching for us.

In November 2008, we started a blog to share food cooked for friends, family, and ourselves. In a short time, the site transformed into an interactive platform with thousands of readers. In the beginning, we did not think about how our unique methods of cooking would evolve and what food would come to mean to us. That first post—pumpkin pie—was influenced by family traditions but with our own spin. Cardamom, amaretto, and a dash of cayenne for the filling, and nutty wheat germ in the homemade graham crust created a pie different from the ones we may have had before. Our cooking evolution had begun.

We grew up in dissimilar ways. Amir had a large family, and I was an only child. Although the action around the dinner table varied immensely between my quiet home in New Jersey and Amir's busier childhood homes in Illinois and North Carolina, we both grew up appreciating food prepared at home.

That being said, the types of things that we ate on an average night were very different. Being health-conscious physicians, Amir's parents prepared wholesome meals, making sure dinner was well balanced and nutritious. They left the grocery store with foods that were minimally processed and free of superfluous sodium and sugar. On the other hand, I came from a family of cooking convenience. We had canned vegetables, sauces, and dressings to accompany baked chicken or pork chops, pasta, and bagged salads. There were nights of Chinese take-out or cereal for dinner if no one felt like whipping up a meal. Even though the foods we ate in our respective families were different, it was always important in both of our homes that the family would sit down together to eat.

After college and separate moves across the country, Amir and I each developed our own style of cooking. Amir replicated his favorite dishes from home, using memory and taste as the main guides. I began to appreciate the taste of year-round fresh produce, herbs and spices, and preparing sauces and dressings from scratch. We both enjoyed walking through local farmers' markets and pawing grocery store aisles for new ingredients to add flavor to our foods. We often think about how, in those days, we were most likely eating very differently from the majority of African Americans in their late 20s, but since then we have "virtually" friended like-minded African American food bloggers and cooks who have embraced organic, seasonal goods from local farmers' markets, or even grow their own simple herbs in their small backyards.

As young urbanites, we may not have the space to grow vegetables and fruits like our ancestors, but we can easily pop a tiny herb garden onto the balcony or patio. We have also discovered the bounty available through Community Supported Agriculture organizations and directories. Being in touch with our food has most definitely affected the way we cook, as well as the cooking styles of many other young African Americans who strive to be more involved with the ingredients they use. The online community has responded positively to the ways we have taken recipes and made them our own.

We enjoy new tastes, textures, and creations, but we also love the simpler foods from our pasts. Adding a modern spin on the traditional is inspiring and enriching for us. We eat in the "in-between"—a place where what we love to cook rises from roots and creates new paths.

Amir and I have found that the way we move through the kitchen and develop unique recipes has been appreciated by our readers. We are often "applauded" for exploring neighborhood ethnic markets, investigating new flavors, and testing various means of fusion. Perhaps our readers will feel a bit less hesitant about their forays in the kitchen once they've seen our success—and even our failures. We do not attempt to hide any gaffes that may occur, as we believe that the good and the bad are both part of creating a meal. In the end, it's our ability to stay true to our style of cooking, whether learned under the tutelage of grandmother or influenced by the televised words of Paula Deen, that allows us to stay true to ourselves.

What we both share is a strong love for food and cooking that has made us passionate eaters. It is that passion and interest that shapes how we have evolved and will continue to evolve. With food, we will carry on many of the traditions ingrained from years past as we forge on to create our own.

The Duo Dishes' Honey Dijon Spiced Pecan Coleslaw

Los Angeles, California

SERVES 6 TO 8

There is very little mayonnaise in this coleslaw, but that is more than made up for by the combination of spices that are used.

½ medium red onion, minced
16 ounces shredded cabbage
1 carrot, shredded
¼ cup Dijon mustard
1 tablespoon mayonnaise
1 tablespoon apple cider vinegar
⅓ cup honey
zest and juice of ½ lemon
1 teaspoon caraway seeds or celery seeds (optional)
½ cup pecans, chopped
½ tablespoon brown sugar
½ tablespoon white sugar
½ tablespoon unsalted butter
½ teaspoon cayenne pepper
¼ cup dried cranberries
kosher salt

Mix onion, cabbage, and carrot in a large bowl.

In a separate, smaller bowl, whisk mustard, mayonnaise, vinegar, honey, lemon juice and zest, and caraway seeds. Season to taste with salt. Pour dressing over coleslaw mix. Toss well then chill in the fridge.

As slaw chills, add butter to a pan. When melted, toss in pecans. Sprinkle with cayenne and brown sugar and toss to coat. Slide onto parchment paper- or wax paper-covered sheet and pop in the freezer until completely cooled.

When ready to serve, add spiced pecans and cranberries to slaw and toss to combine.

The Duo Dishes' Cornbread Panzanella

Los Angeles, California

SERVES 4 TO 6

This salad turns cornbread, an everyday staple in soul food cooking, into an elegant, Italian-inspired salad.

3 cups leftover cornbread (page 42), cubed
1 tablespoon unsalted butter
1 pint mixed cherry tomatoes, halved
1 medium red onion, diced
1 cucumber, peeled, deseeded, and diced
10–15 fresh basil leaves, sliced
⅓ cup olive oil
¼ cup balsamic vinegar
½ tablespoon Dijon mustard
zest of 1 lemon
1 tablespoon maple syrup
kosher salt

Melt butter in an oven-safe pan or heavy skillet and add cornbread. Toss cornbread in butter and cook over medium high heat for 3–5 minutes. Toast in a preheated oven at 300° F for 10–15 minutes or until dry and hard like croutons. Remove from oven and set aside until cool.

Whisk together olive oil, balsamic vinegar, mustard, zest, and maple syrup. Salt to taste.

In a large bowl, toss cornbread with tomatoes, onion, cucumber, and basil. Drizzle with ⅓ to ½ of the dressing and serve the rest on the side.

CHAPTER

2

Baked Goods

··· Rufus Estes ···

Source: Public Domain

Rufus Estes was born eight years before the end of slavery, in Murray County, Tennessee. In 1867, after Emancipation, he and his mother moved to Nashville, where he attended a term of school before having to work to help his ailing mother. He was just 10 years old. By the time he was 16 he got a job working in a Nashville restaurant and two years later found his way to the Pullman Company as one of hundreds of black workers who served as porters, cooks, and janitors on the railway cars that criss-crossed the country.

It was as a Pullman cook that Mr. Estes gained a reputation for culinary skill. His way with food was so prized that he cooked for (or "cared for," as he said in his own words) two presidents, royalty, and famous actresses, composers, and explorers of the day. His book Good Things to Eat *is a compilation of his famous recipes published in his own words in 1911. It is possibly the earliest published cookbook by an African American man and to this day remains a canon of good things to eat.*

"One of the pleasures in life to the normal man is good eating, and if it be true that real happiness consists in making others happy, the author can at least feel a sense of gratification in the thought that his attempts to satisfy the cravings of the inner man have not been wholly unappreciated by the many that he has had the pleasure of serving—some of whom are now his stanchest friends. In fact, it was in response to the insistence and encouragement of these friends that he embarked on the rather hazardous undertaking of offering this collection to a discriminating public."

— from the Foreword to *Good Things to Eat*, Rufus Estes, 1911.

These three recipes, adapted from *Good Things to Eat*, make use of three types of corn that were and are a staple in the soul food kitchen.

Rufus Estes' Hominy Cake

SERVES 4

2 cups of boiled hominy
2 tablespoons of melted butter
1 egg, beaten
⅓ teaspoon salt
1 teaspoon black pepper
¼ cup finely grated cheddar or Parmesan cheese

Preheat oven to 250° F. Using a fork, smash the cooked hominy into fine pieces. Alternatively, pulse the cooked hominy in a food processor until fine.

Mix the hominy with eggs, salt, and pepper. Stir well until combined.

Form the mixture into small patties about 3 inches wide. Place in a buttered baking dish large enough to hold all the patties in one layer. Sprinkle with grated cheese and bake 25–30 minutes or until just golden brown.

Serve hot.

Rufus Estes' Southern Corncake

MAKES 1 CAKE

2 cups white cornmeal
1 tablespoon sugar
1 teaspoon salt
¾ cup hot milk, or more as needed
3 eggs, beaten

Preheat oven to 350° F. Mix cornmeal, sugar, and salt together in a bowl.

Add milk to moisten the mixture to a soft dough. Beat in eggs and mix well.

Spread mixture into a greased 8 x 12 baking dish and bake until firm, about 30 minutes. Remove and cool slightly. Cut into squares and serve warm with butter.

Mr. Estes' Corn Fritters

MAKES 10 FRITTERS

1 cup corn niblets, chopped finely
½ cup flour
½ teaspoon baking powder
1 teaspoon salt
¼ teaspoon cayenne pepper
1 egg, separated
½ cup canola oil

Mix the corn, flour, baking powder, salt, and cayenne in a bowl. Add egg yolk and mix well.

Beat egg white to stiff peaks and fold that into the corn mixture.

Heat oil in a wide, deep frying pan until it reaches 350° F or until a pinch of flour dropped into the oil bubbles.

Drop the corn dough mixture into the hot oil by the tablespoonful, turning once while cooking so they are lightly brown on both sides, about 2 minutes per side.

Drain fritters on a wire rack set over a cookie sheet or sheet tray, or on a paper towel-lined plate.

Serve warm with your favorite condiments.

• •

Pass It Down tip: *These corn fritters make a great appetizer. Make them special by serving with a side of Remoulade Sauce (page 231) and garnishing with some freshly chopped parsley.*

• •

Monkey Bread à la Bailey

Detroit, Michigan

SERVES 6

Roderick Woodruff confirms that his beloved Aunt Zanola Bailey has been the keeper of the most trusted family recipes for decades. Indeed, no holiday can officially begin without the delicious smells of fresh bread baking in the oven. The casting of the monkey bread magic spell was bequeathed to Zanola by her father, Bruce Bailey, a master chef who planted a great love for family celebrations, joyous holidays, and good food in all of his descendants.

2 yeast cakes (or packages)
1 cup boiled and finely mashed sweet potatoes
1 cup sugar
½ cup warm water
2 sticks of butter
1 cup milk
1½ teaspoons salt
3 large eggs and 2 egg yolks
6–7 cups of flour

Place 2 yeast cakes in a large bowl. Mix well with 1 cup of sugar and ½ cup of warm water. Wait to see little bubbles appear—ensures that yeast is active! Divide butter in half. Place one stick in a bowl near the stove to soften and melt. Place the other stick in a pan with 1 cup milk and add 1½ teaspoons of salt. Bring mixture to a scald.

In another bowl, beat the 3 eggs and 2 yolks slightly. Combine with yeast and sugar mixture. Mix well with wooden spoon. Add milk, butter, and salt mixture. Mix well with above.

Add flour cup by cup until mixture appears lumpy. Continue until the consistency is enough to place on bread board. Knead in the remaining flour plus a little more for 10 minutes. Place this in a large buttered bowl and cover with a plastic wrap until contents have doubled in size.

Punch down with fingers. For lighter bread allow it to rise a second time. Pull off piece by piece and layer them in a Bundt cake pan. Dip each piece in butter before placing in tube pan.

Bake at 350° F for 45 minutes to an hour. Color should be golden brown. Serve from the oven with honey butter or with butter and jelly for a special treat.

Patricia Lynch's Buttermilk Cornbread

Oakland, California

MAKES 1 DISH

Mississippi native Patricia A. Lynch is the mother of one and an outstanding grandmother. She is also an expert cook who enjoys hosting functions for her family, friends, and church members. She says this savory cornbread is ideal for stuffing and dressing like Ms. Burrell's Four State Oyster Dressing on page 106.

½ cup chopped onions
¼ cup chopped bell peppers
1 stalks celery, chopped
2 garlic cloves, minced
1½ cups yellow cornmeal
1 cup flour
2 teaspoons baking powder
¼ teaspoon baking soda
pinch of salt and pepper
⅓ teaspoon seasoning salt
⅓ teaspoon celery salt
2 large eggs
½ stick butter, melted
1 cup of buttermilk

Preheat oven to 425° F. Preheat an 8x8 baking dish, or large iron skillet in the oven.

Sauté the vegetables in 1 tablespoon of butter until translucent. Do not allow them to brown.

Mix the corn meal, flour, baking powder, baking soda, salt, pepper, seasoning salt, and celery salt in a large bowl.

Mix the eggs, butter, and buttermilk together in a separate bowl, and add them to the cornmeal mixture. Beat well and add the onions, bell peppers, celery and garlic.

Add 3–4 tablespoons of canola oil to the baking dish or iron skillet. Pour the batter into either the baking dish or pan. Bake until golden brown, about 15–20 minutes or until a cake tester stuck in the middle of the bread comes out clean.

··· **Ironic Authority** ···

African American Images in Food Advertising

BY MICHELE Y. WASHINGTON

Source: Library of Congress

Source: Library of Congress

*Michele Y. Washington is a design critic, writer, and researcher interested in expanding the discourse in cross-cultural design and the role architecture, urbanism, visual and material culture, and fashion play in our everyday lives. She maintains a design consultancy in NYC and a blog that focuses on her research in cross-cultural research at **culturalboundaries.com/wordpress/**.*

In 1991 I co-curated an exhibition in which African American designers challenged modern stereotypes. Each graphic designer was charged with the task to create a one-of-kind poster addressing how blacks have been continuously portrayed in the media. I decided to tackle the image of Aunt Jemima by creating a poster I called "Ain't Ja Mama on the Pancake Box." As I researched my piece, I began to think deeply about the image of the heavy-set, wide-bosomed black woman, hair tied up and grinning from ear to ear. She was a soothing, even comforting figure in American food advertising. Pancakes, after all, are homey, cozy, sweet, and delicate.

The truth is, of course, that Aunt Jemima is just one of the poor mammy, pickaninny, and blackface characters who were a standard portrayal of Africa Americans—one that was used to peddle everything from tires to clothing to food.

Toni Tipton-Martin, a food historian, has extensively researched the origins of such symbolic black figures and contrasted their existence with a lack of respect and recognition given to black cooks and their integral role in America's culinary arts. It's a bitter irony that black cooks' success has always been dependent on the authority invested in these figures. Aunt Jemima, Uncle Ben, and their offspring are experts in their "fields" and that's what makes their products good.

It is an irony that was played out over and over in, among a myriad of places, the pages of popular magazines. Aunt Jemima, for example was portrayed as the expert teacher from whom the modern housewife could learn a thing or two in a 1927 *McCall's* magazine ad. "Have you tried her ingredients?" goes the tagline. By 1940, she appeared in *Woman's Day* as a dating counselor, advising a young woman to make flapjacks with her easy mix as a way of getting her man to stay for dinner.

A fictitious character conjured by two white businessmen, Charles L. Rutt and Charles G. Underwood, to sell pancake mix, the Aunt Jemima character is loosely based on Vaudevillian blackface, whose characters had glaring red painted lips and crazed eyes meant to indicate their wild, unintelligent demeanors. In the flesh, real women portrayed Aunt Jemima at fairs and expositions, starting with Nancy Green, born a slave. Clever marketers, Rutt and Charles knew that the authority and believability of the character was absolutely dependent on the ring of authenticity.

Mars, the company that owns Uncle Ben's Converted Rice, has always been hushed about their "spokesperson." Uncle Ben was created in 1943 and his backstory has at times suggested that he was a respected rice farmer, although that was never directly depicted in any marketing materials. Yet the name "uncle" specifically relates to the habit of referring to older black men in a form of pseudo respect, since they were not worthy of the term "mister" but their age dictated some deference. Again, the irony of authority is bizarrely played out: It was slaves from the African rice coast (See the essay Bitter Grains, page 167) who had the heritage knowledge to keep the lucrative rice plantation culture going. Indeed, an "uncle" of Ben's caliber would have exactly been the most dependable authority on rice.

Perhaps the most offensive of the holdovers is the black chef that still graces boxes of Cream of Wheat. His name is Rastus, a long-accepted pejorative for a particular type of dumb minstrel character. Yet even while the character is branded with an insulting name, he wears a chef's coat and hat and, in fact, was drawn using a photo portrait of Frank White, a Barbados-born, African American master chef who worked in Chicago.

This bizarre juxtaposition of authority and scorn is just one of the reasons why Ms. Tipton-Martin created the Jemima Code, an online project documenting her research into black images in advertising. She reminds us that each of these characters might easily represent the memories of our parents or grandparents, who at one time might have worked as cooks in the kitchens of prominent hotels or restaurants, as waiters on trains, or domestics in prominent homes or even in the White House.

Fast forward to today, when all three characters have undergone a redesign: Aunt Jemima is owned by Quaker Oats and went from mammy to hyper-stylized in the 1990s, losing her robust figure, jolly facial features, and now sporting free-flowing, seemingly relaxed hair. Rastus still beckons you with his welcoming smile, offering steamy hot cereal to comfort a child's tummy. While his style is almost unchanged, his chef jacket appears structured with a more stylish ascot rather than floppy bow tie. Uncle Ben, still without a surname, has stepped into the 21st century. No longer fully viewed by his subservient cultural identity, he's been promoted to chairman in the board room. In a *New York Times* article discussing the updated Uncle Ben, actual chairman Vincent Howell, president of the food division of the Masterfoods, USA unit of Mars, said he found the new and improved Uncle Ben to be a powerful image of an African American in a figure of prominence and authority—especially as an African American himself. Unfortunately, Uncle Ben's style makers failed to erase his royal blue jacket and crisp white shirt and dowdy bow tie—cultural expressions still linking him to his past as a waiter or Pullman porter.

What's puzzling is why American culture remains attached to outmoded icons to represent some of its most popular food brands. When they were originally introduced, they were a gentler depiction of an accepted "truth" of African American culture. Yet as each year passes, such icons must not remain cast as invisible men and women. In the 21st century they should be recognized as polarizing symbols that reinforce a culture unwilling to part with certain "benign" stereotypes. Hidden in the boxes of bland cereal, sweet pancake mix, and fluffy rice is a history, not just of scorn, but of a far greater injury: authority given lightly with one hand and snatched back with the other.

Dr. Carver's Sweet Potato Biscuits

Tuskegee, Alabama

MAKES 12 BISCUITS

This truly delicious recipe for sweet potato biscuits appeared in How the Farmer Can Save His Sweet Potatoes and Ways of Preparing Them for the Table *by Dr. George Washington Carver (Reprinted by Texas AfriLife Extension Service, Bulletin No. 38 (First edition) November 1922).*

2 cups flour
2 teaspoons baking powder
1 teaspoon salt
1 tablespoon sugar (if desired)
2 scant tablespoons melted butter or lard
2 cups milk
2 eggs, well beaten
1 cup boiled and finely mashed sweet potatoes

Mix together all the dry ingredients and stir into the milk, beaten eggs, and potato.

If too soft, add more flour, sufficient to make a soft dough.

Roll out lightly; cut with a biscuit cutter; bake in a quick oven until golden brown.

Dwight Jones' Cream Biscuits

St. Louis, Missouri

MAKES 12 BISCUITS

Dwight Jones is an engineer, chef, barbecue pit master, hunter, and fisherman—and a skilled pastry chef. His cream biscuits are a luxurious take on traditional baking powder biscuits. And while you can substitute buttermilk or even plain milk for the cream, the White Lily flour, he says, is non-negotiable.

2 cups White Lily all-purpose flour
½ teaspoon salt
3 teaspoons baking powder
6 tablespoons unsalted butter, cut into small pieces
1 cup heavy cream

Preheat oven to 425° F.

Mix dry ingredients together in a medium bowl. Add butter and incorporate until mixture resembles coarse sand.

Add cream and mix until soft dough just starts to form. Do not over mix.

Turn dough out on a floured surface and knead just until the firm ball of dough forms. Roll the dough into a ½-inch-thick disc. Cut biscuits with a 2½-inch round cutter.

Place on a lightly greased baking sheet and place in the oven for approximately 15 minutes or until golden brown.

Serve hot.

• •

I cast my bread on the waters long ago. Now it's time for you to send it back to me— toasted and buttered on both sides.

— The Reverend Jesse Jackson

• •

Jane Nganga's Maandazi

Rancho Cucamonga, California

MAKES ABOUT 15

Maandazi is one of a group of East African fried breads that can be savory or slightly sweet, as this one is. It is most often eaten for breakfast. Similar fried breads that are moistened with coconut milk are called mamri.

10 cardamom pods, or ½ teaspoon powdered cardamom
5 cups self-rising flour
⅛ teaspoon castor sugar
¾ tablespoon baking powder
¼ teaspoon cumin
1 teaspoon snipped chives
1 large egg
2 tablespoons canola or peanut oil
2 cups milk
10 cups canola or peanut oil for deep frying

If using whole cardamom, crush the cardamom pods in mortar and pestle and shake out the seeds. Grind seeds in the mortar to a powder and place it in a large bowl with flour, castor sugar, baking powder, cumin, and chives.

Beat egg and 2 tablespoons of oil together in a small bowl and add them to the flour mixture. Using your fingertips, mix well, then add the milk slowly to make a soft, firm dough.

Knead dough lightly until smooth and not sticky, and allow to rest, covered in a warm place for 30 minutes.

Roll out the dough on a floured surface to about ½-inch thickness and use a 3-inch round pastry cutter to cut out 15 rounds.

Heat the 10 cups of oil in a deep pot until it reaches 350° F or until a pinch of flour dropped into the oil bubbles vigorously.

Fry 4–5 minutes, flipping over once, or until donuts turn golden. Serve as a snack or an accompaniment to a meal.

Tater Pie

Chestertown, Maryland

MAKES 1 PIE

Hilda Hopkins was born in 1926 of mixed black, white, and Native American ancestry, and grew up on Maryland's shore. She recalls that her mixed heritage meant that racism came from all sides. Life was often hard, especially being one of twelve children. Tater pie was a go-to dish her mother made when there was little or no food in the house. "My special memory is that my mother always said, 'It's time to make tater pie,'" says Ms. Hopkins. "She would bake five or six of these pies and it was all we had to eat for the day."

1 pound of white baking potatoes, boiled and peeled
1 stick of butter, softened
1½ cups sugar
½ teaspoon salt
2 eggs, separated
1 can evaporated milk
1 teaspoon vanilla extract
½ teaspoon lemon extract
1 piecrust

Preheat oven to 350° F.

Cut potatoes into chunks and place them in a mixer with the butter. Add sugar and salt, and mix on medium until smooth.

Add egg yolks one at a time and mix until well combined. Add milk, vanilla extract, and lemon extract.

In a separate bowl, whip egg whites to a stiff peak and gently fold into the potato batter.

Pour the batter into the piecrust. Bake 45 minutes or until the top is golden brown and a cake tester stuck into the middle of the pie comes out clean.

Sylvia Barton's Spoon Bread

SERVES 6 TO 8

Sylvia Barton with her sons
Craig and (Chef) Scott.

Scott Alves Barton is a noted chef, culinary historian, and lover of food culture. When he's not cooking or teaching cooking to both adults and kids, he's following the threads of culinary culture around the world, weaving them into the fine fabric of history and heritage. His greatest inspiration in food, he says, was his mother Sylvia Alves Barton, an outstanding educator and nutritionist whose aspirations in the 1930s to be a chef as a young New Yorker, although not realized in her own life, have been satisfyingly fulfilled in the life of her son.

His mother took inspiration from her West Indian heritage as well as her husband's roots, which touched New England. "In the last few years, I've lost my mom and recently lost my dad too," says Chef Barton, "so the legacy she gave us in delighting to be at home in the kitchen is a gift that has taken on a much deeper meaning."

2 cups milk
3 tablespoons unsalted butter
1 cup stone-ground white cornmeal
4 large eggs, separated
¼ cup freshly grated grana padano cheese
salt and cayenne pepper to taste
6 4-ounce crocks or 1 9-inch loaf pan, buttered and floured with cornmeal

Preheat oven to 375° F. Place milk and butter in medium saucepan set on medium-high heat. When the mixture comes just to a boil, remove from the heat.

Whisk in the cornmeal in a steady stream to avoid lumps. Place mixture in a large bowl and set aside.

Whisk the whites to soft peaks. Fold the yolks and cheese into cornmeal mixture, then gently fold in the whites.

Pour batter into the prepared pan or pans and bake 12–15 minutes until a thin-bladed knife or cake tester comes out slightly moist.

Serve warm as a delicious appetizer or as a side dish to accompany braised meats, hearty stews, or as a special treat for company or Sunday dinner.

CHAPTER 3

Poultry & Meats

Craig Robinson's Mom's Buttermilk Fried Chicken

Los Angeles, California

SERVES 4 TO 6

Craig Robinson describes his father as African American and his mother as French and black. Mrs. Robinson was, her son says, an avid cook and foodie years before the Food Network, and was ahead of the curve and always trying new, healthy recipes. "My mother was doing California Cuisine before the term existed," he says. "As a child I never really experienced 'soul food' in my house. I primarily enjoyed Italian, French, and Lebanese cuisines growing up in my household." Despite her experimental attitude, his mother's old-fashioned fried chicken is one of the things he most misses since she passed away from breast cancer in 2005. Plus, he recalls, "Those Food TV chefs had nothing on my moms. She had the look, personality, and—most important—she could cook!"

1 3-pound fryer chicken, cut into eight pieces
2 cups buttermilk
6 cloves garlic, smashed
1 large onion, sliced
1 cup chopped mixed fresh herbs (parsley, tarragon, thyme)
½ teaspoon paprika
1 teaspoon cayenne pepper
2 cups flour
¼ teaspoon garlic salt
¼ teaspoon onion salt
salt and pepper
3 cups solid vegetable shortening

Soak chicken in buttermilk with garlic, onions, herbs, paprika, and ½ teaspoon of the cayenne pepper. Refrigerate overnight.

Place chicken pieces in a colander to drain.

In a large paper bag, mix flour with the garlic salt, onion salt, salt and pepper, and remaining ½ teaspoon of cayenne pepper. Meanwhile, heat the 3 cups of shortening in a deep cast iron pot until it's about 350° F.

Place chicken pieces in bag with flour and shake, let sit 1 minute, and then shake again. Add chicken to hot pan and fry on one side for 20 minutes, then turn and fry on the other side for 15 minutes more.

Place chicken pieces on a wire rack set over a cookie tray to drain, or on a paper towel-lined plate.

● ●

Pass It Down variation: *Preheat oven to 400˚ F. Substitute plain crumbs for flour in the breading. Grease a large, ovenproof dish. Layer the chicken pieces in the baking dish in one layer. Brush the top of the chicken lightly with cooking oil, cover loosely with foil, and bake for 20 minutes. Remove foil and bake 20 minutes more.*

● ●

Craig Robinson's mother's recipe for fried chicken is, he says, "old skool"—using vegetable shortening rather than oil. For a lighter, healthier version (without the trans fat of shortening), fry the chicken pieces using 1 cup of canola oil in a large fry pan. Turn chicken pieces once they're lightly browned on one side, about 15 minutes, then turn and brown the other side, about 15 minutes more. Remove the chicken pieces from the pan and place them on a wire rack set over a cookie sheet or sheet tray and bake in a 400˚ F oven for 20 more minutes more. This will allow the oil to drip off the chicken while it continues to cook—while staying crispy!

Calvetta McGill's Finger Lickin' Southern Fried Chicken

Wildwood, Florida

SERVES 4 TO 6

Source: Wendy McGill

Calvetta McGill hopes to one day pass this recipe down to her now-infant son. It was handed to her from her great-aunt. "Each time I visited her as a child, this is what she prepared and it tasted better each time." Ms. McGill's method requires covering the pot, which many folks feel leads to a truly tender fried chicken.

1 large fryer (about 3 pounds) cut into 8 pieces
2 tablespoons yellow mustard
1 tablespoon brown vinegar
½ teaspoon salt (or to taste)
½ teaspoon black pepper (or to taste)
½ teaspoon cayenne pepper (or to taste)
2 cups canola oil
2 cups flour

Wash the chicken in cold water. Place in a glass bowl with the mustard, vinegar, salt, and peppers. Mix well until every piece of chicken is well coated. Cover with plastic wrap and refrigerate overnight.

Heat the oil in a large deep skillet until it reaches about 350° F or until a pinch of flour tossed into the oil bubbles vigorously.

While oil is heating, remove chicken from the refrigerator and dredge lightly in the flour.

Place the chicken pieces in the hot oil and cover with the lid. Lower heat to medium-high and fry chicken pieces for 20 minutes, turning once and frying 20 minutes more or until golden brown and cooked through.

Jessica B. Harris' Touchstone Chicken Yassa

New Orleans, Louisiana

SERVES 6

Source: Kristy May

Jessica B. Harris is a historian of African and African American foodways, a calling that has led her around the globe and to publishing multiple books. She is the first Ray Charles Chair in African American Material Culture at Dillard University in New Orleans and has been granted several prestigious awards for her work. She calls this Senegalese dish, learned on a research trip for her book Iron Pots & Wooden Spoons, *which covered the foodways of Africans in the Diaspora, her "touchstone." It is, she writes, "The first dish I tasted and truly enjoyed."*

¼ cup freshly squeezed lemon juice
4 large onions, sliced
salt and freshly ground pepper, to taste
5 tablespoons peanut oil
1 habañero chile
1 frying chicken (2½ to 4½ pounds) cut into serving pieces
½ cup water

The night before, prepare a marinade by mixing the lemon juice, onions, salt, pepper, and 4 tablespoons of the peanut oil in a deep bowl. Prick the chile with the tines of a fork and add it to the marinade as well. When the dish has reached the desired degree of hotness, remove the chile and reserve (it can be minced and served separately to the chile heads).

Place the chicken pieces in the marinade, cover with plastic wrap, and refrigerate overnight (if you are pressed for time you can marinate for two hours, but the flavor won't be as intense).

When ready to cook, preheat the boiler. Remove the chicken pieces from the marinade, reserving the marinade and the onions. Place the pieces on the broiler rack and grill them briefly, until they are just lightly browned on both sides. Set aside.

Drain the onions from the marinade. Heat the remaining tablespoon of oil in a deep skillet and sauté the onions over medium heat until they are tender and translucent. Add the remaining marinade and cook until the liquid is heated through. Add the chicken pieces and the water and stir to mix well.

Lower the heat and simmer, covered, until the chicken pieces are cooked through, at least 30 minutes. Serve the yassa over white rice.

··· Great Migrations ···

BY DONNA DANIELS

Dr. Donna Daniels is a cultural anthropologist and market researcher who specializes in African American studies.

". . . Like my grandmother and other African American families adapting to a large Northern city amidst the second Great Migration, my parents stuck close to home—shopping for pork chops, ham hocks, and ground beef at the local butcher, and buying the fruits and vegetables of their childhood from a stand on Girard Avenue in Philadelphia. They stayed well within the boundaries of their own neighborhood and shopped among people who looked as they did."

It was a day in 1969. I don't recall the month so I don't know the season. Whether we were eating Jersey tomatoes or Pennsylvania Dutch Country apples escapes me. What I do recall are the details of the pronouncement.

"I'm going to make lasagna," my older sister, Deborah, informed my family.

It was as if someone had run a needle across Sly and the Family Stone's "Everyday People" to abruptly bring an end to a house party. My father looked up from his *Scientific American*, puzzled, if not stunned. My mother carefully leaned her broom against the stairwell wall and took a seat near him at our white, octagonal Formica dining room table. I stood at our back door, hand on the door handle. I was seven years old and ready to go out to play. But I stayed glued to the spot because I knew, somehow, that something big had just happened.

"An Italian girl from my home ec. class brought in a recipe for her grandmother's lasagna," Deborah continued, "and I want to try it. You have to use fresh garlic when you make the meat sauce. So I'll need to buy some things like the garlic, Parmesan cheese, dried basil . . ."

If silence is golden, then a very deep amber light had just flooded our small Philadelphia row house. Debbie, my parents' pride and joy and, at age fifteen, their dependably compliant daughter, had just violated a rule that ordered our home and, for that matter, my mother's kitchen: the rule of cultural insularity.

My parents grew up in the segregated South, my mother in Alabama, my father in North Carolina. They met at North Carolina A&T University, each the first in their family to go to college. In 1949, a few years after graduation, they married and settled in North Philadelphia, joining my paternal grandmother. And like my grandmother and other African American families adapting to a large Northern city amidst the second Great Migration, they stuck close to home—shopping for pork chops, ham hocks, and ground beef at the local butcher, and buying the fruits and vegetables of their childhood from a stand on Girard Avenue in Philadelphia. They stayed well within the boundaries of their own neighborhood and shopped among people who looked as they did.

It didn't take long for my mother to fall for Philadelphia. She loved its revolutionary history, its cobblestone streets, its cracked Liberty Bell, its spirit of independence. But the love affair was not without its challenges. For both my father, an electrical engineer, and my mother, who had studied to be a teacher, it took longer than they'd imagined to find employment.

My parents made sure we understood that racial discrimination had stalled and delayed each of their careers. Add to that the limits of brotherly love in 1950s Philly, its neighborhoods shaped by a stark ethnic geography, and you had two recent somewhat shell-shocked transplants who were wary of Italian, Polish, and German areas, and who avoided the unfamiliar, from stores to people. My parents traversed

Philadelphia with a deliberateness aimed at dodging the sting of a racial epithet and staying out of harm's way. By sticking close to home and sticking to the familiar, they believed we would all be safe.

And yet, intentionally or otherwise, they had put their children on a different path. They raised us as the children of integration, and as such, we believed that all of Philadelphia belonged to us.

So, on a Saturday morning some time after the Great Lasagna Declaration, we piled into our blue VW bug and drove to 9th Street to the Italian Market. Deborah had lobbied for this day and now it was here, though the road had been long and parental resistance had been fierce.

"The Italian market, in South Philly?" my father had asked. "A market for Italians? That's where you need to go for garlic? Sport (my mother's nickname), are you hearing this?"

"It's not for Italians," my sister said, throwing up her hands in exasperation, "anyone can go there."

"Can't we get garlic at the A & P, Debbie? Surely we don't have to go all over creation for it. Besides, I still don't see why you can't use garlic salt or the powder." My mother was irritated.

With my parents clearly intent on treating travel to South Philadelphia like a trip to the moon, my sister realized that she needed to call in reinforcements. They came in the form of Madelyn Crocker, our intrepid next-door neighbor. Eastern shore of Maryland-born and city savvy, Mrs. Crocker knew Philadelphia like the back of her hand, and it seemed she had been everywhere within its city limits at least twice. She had the ability to charm my parents. Conspiring with my sister, in a lilting voice that was both mannered and direct, she explained that everyone and their brother could be found at the market, even "colored people."

As soon as we were parked, my sister, barely containing her excitement, leapt out of the car.

"Slow down," my mother called nervously as she ran to catch up, apprehension and curiosity animating her face. My father and I trailed behind, his hand firmly grasping mine as we neared the bustling street.

"There are a lot of us here," my father mused under his breath.

He seemed to relax. Soon we were picking through the produce of overflowing stands, entering stores with their strange smells and stranger products, part of the throng of people enjoying the ritual of shopping outdoors. In the car on the way home, I assessed my sister's bounty. I had never seen garlic up close. Its white, papery skin was smooth to the touch. My sister pointed out its individual cloves and whispered that she would have to peel and chop them for the sauce. We traveled across Philadelphia reflecting on our journey. It would prove to be the first of many Saturdays at the Italian market.

The smell of the lasagna fresh out of the oven filled our small row house. My mother reported to my father that she had only shadowed my sister while she prepared the dish.

"Deborah made it all by herself," she beamed. "She chopped the garlic, made the sauce, cooked those noodles, even grated the cheese like she's been making this for years."

My mother may have been a little wistful. She was, after all, my sister's original cooking teacher, instructing her in the African American Southern style of cooking. Now my sister had taken those basics and run with them, all the way to another continent.

"Enjoy," Deborah said after serving us a portion of her masterpiece, a look of pride lighting up her face. When we each asked for seconds, her triumph was clear. Lasagna would become her signature dish. She would take requests from relatives and friends, toting her Pyrex of Italian goodness to all manner of parties and special occasions. She made it for us at least once a month.

In September of 1971, a month before her 17th birthday, my sister died. A brain tumor struck her down and laid my family low. Perhaps because in my grief the longing to be like my big sister intensified, it didn't take me long to find my way into the kitchen. By the time I was in junior high, I could whip up a lasagna—fresh garlic and all—using my sister's recipe and bringing Deborah's memory to the table.

Italian food, it turned out, was just the beginning for my culinary explorations. I would take my mother's Southern approach to cooking all over the world—seasoning meat ahead of time; seeking out fresh fruits and vegetables even if it meant growing your own; appreciating the joys of chit'lin's, pigs' feet, and other cheap cuts of meat, known in the high-end food world as "offal"; and knowing that homemade cornbread makes most meals better. And in the spirit of my sister I would seek out unfamiliar ingredients for recipes from India, Thailand, China, Japan, Sri Lanka, France, Spain, Puerto Rico, Jamaica, Brazil, Senegal, Ghana, Ethiopia, and most recently Poland (love will take you places you'd never expect). I'm a restless cook. Who knows where I'll go next? I just know that wherever I go, my mother and sister will be with me.

Donna Daniels' Sumac Roast Chicken

Guilford, Connecticut

SERVES 4 TO 6

Heart
&
Soul

Source: Donna Daniels

To cultural anthropologist Dr. Donna Daniels, roast chicken is both a Sunday meal and a comfort meal. She says she has taken this dish in many directions over the years—making it with an Asian influence using soy sauce and sesame oil along with garlic and onion, as well as using parsley, scallions, shallots, and roasted garlic as a variation of her mom's recipe. Lately, sumac has entered the anthropologist's spice cabinet thanks to her interest in flavors from North Africa and the Middle East. "I learned to love spice and seasoning from my mother and am always expanding my knowledge and experience. Roast chicken is always a favored canvas for me to try something new," she says.

1 tablespoon kosher salt or to taste
2½ teaspoons fresh ground pepper or to taste
1 heaping tablespoon ground sumac, available in Middle Eastern stores*
2 teaspoons urfa chile or Aleppo pepper available in Middle Eastern stores*
1 4- to 5-pound chicken, preferably organic
5 large cloves of garlic, sliced thinly
10–12 thyme sprigs
3 large shallots chopped
¼ cup olive oil

Preheat oven to 425° F.

Make a spice rub with salt, pepper, sumac, and urfa chile. Rub spice mixture under the skin of the chicken, taking care to season the breast and the legs well. Also rub some of the mixture inside chicken as well as on top of the skin.

Slide garlic slices, thyme sprigs, and chopped shallots under skin and in cavity. Rub chicken all over with olive oil and place in a roasting pan.

---

* Ground sumac can also be purchased online from Penzey's spices, **www.penzeys.com**, or Kalustyan's in New York or online, **www.kalustyans.com.** Urfa chile can also be purchased from Kalustyan's.

Roast chicken for 50–70 minutes, depending on size of bird. Begin with the breast side up, then turn chicken over about 30 minutes into cooking and baste with pan drippings every 20 minutes for the first hour.

Turn the bird over again so the breast side is up for the last 15 minutes of roasting. Insert a meat thermometer between leg and thigh. It should read 165° F. When pierced, the juices that come out of the thigh should be clear, not pink.

- -

Pass It Down variation: Sumac Roast Turkey *This unusual roast chicken makes for a delightfully different Thanksgiving turkey as well. Simply triple the seasonings for a 15-pound bird, or more, proportionate to the bird's weight. For example, multiply seasonings in the recipe by four for a 20-pound bird, by five for a 25-pound bird, and so on.*

- -

Did you know? *Ground sumac was used by the ancient Romans to add sour flavor to dishes—long before they discovered citrus fruits.*

- -

Imani Wilson's Brown Stew Chicken

Queens, New York

SERVES 4 TO 6

When Imani Wilson was four years old, her parents, grandmothers, and aunts started a cookbook for her that she has expanded and added to through her years growing up in Queens, New York, and then as a world-traveling journalist. A writer and ethnomusicologist of Barbadian and Jamaican descent, Ms. Wilson says what she enjoys most about cooking is perfecting the art of combining flavors and textures. Her traditional Jamaican Brown Stew Chicken begins with a caramelized sugar base, believed to be a West African cooking style brought to the Caribbean. Together with the browning, as the caramel foundation is called, allspice, fresh ginger, and Scotch bonnet peppers create an extraordinary depth of flavor to the dish.

1 3-pound chicken cut into eighths plus four additional chicken thighs
juice of 3 limes
⅓ cup kosher salt
4 cups of water
1¼ cups green seasoning (page 232)
¼ cup peanut oil
3 garlic cloves, mashed
10–15 shallots chopped, to yield 1½ cups
½ cup ginger, cut into batons
5 tablespoons Demerara or turbinado sugar
½ cup soy sauce
1 scotch bonnet pepper
1 teaspoon ground or 1 tablespoon whole Jamaican allspice
3 cloves garlic, sliced
sea salt and pepper to taste
½ cup chopped scallion for garnish

Wash the chicken in cold water, then place them in a large, deep bowl or pot and add the lime juice, salt, and three cups of water. Stir the mixture until the salt is dissolved. Set aside, refrigerate for 1 hour.

Remove the chicken from the brine and pat dry. Remove all the skin and fat and set aside.

Add 1 cup of the green seasoning to the chicken and mix to coat. Mix reserved skin with ¼ cup of green seasoning and mix to coat. Allow both mixtures to marinate for an hour.

Place the chicken skin in a cast iron skillet over medium heat. When the fat has been rendered and the skin has fried crisp, remove the skin crackings with a slotted spoon and set them aside. Pour the rendered fat and peanut oil into a large enamel or cast iron Dutch oven and add the chicken. Brown the chicken in a single layer, about 7–8 minutes per side, cooking in batches. Once the chicken pieces have been browned on both sides, remove chicken from pot and set aside on a wire rack set over a sheet tray or a paper towel-lined tray.

Add the mashed garlic, shallots, and ginger to the pan. Fry until the shallots begin to soften, then remove shallot mixture from pan. Sprinkle sugar over bottom of pot and allow to melt. When sugar begins foaming, about 1 minute, add soy sauce, Scotch bonnet, and allspice. Return the shallot mixture to the pot, stirring well to mix.

Return the chicken and any juices to the pot and lower heat to medium-low. Simmer, covered, over medium heat, stirring occasionally. After 45 minutes, remove the Scotch bonnet pepper. Add 1 cup of water and continue cooking for 20 minutes. Add the sliced garlic to the pot. Taste for seasoning and add salt and pepper, as needed. Stir to mix and remove from heat. Let sit for 10 minutes.

Sprinkle the crispy skin and chopped scallions over the stew to serve. Serve with plain rice.

Chicken & Noodles

Columbus, Ohio

SERVES 4 TO 6

Source: Lisa Ghee

Lisa Ghee is a self-professed convenience seeker in the kitchen. She learned this dish from her mom, Constance. It's great taste lies in the simplicity of the ingredients, which include both fresh wholesome ingredients and packaged dry soup mix for added flavor.

1 whole chicken, cut into eighths
3 stalks celery, chopped
1 cup shredded carrots
⅛ teaspoon salt
⅛ teaspoon pepper
⅛ teaspoon allspice
1 package of dry onion soup mix
1 quart chicken stock (page 13)
1 package egg noodles

Preheat oven to 375° F.

Place chicken in Dutch oven or deep roaster and add celery, carrots, salt, pepper, allspice, onion soup mix, and just enough water to cover the chicken pieces by 1 inch.

Cover and cook until chicken is tender, about 1 hour.

Remove the chicken from the roaster and debone. Return the chicken pieces back to the Dutch oven and add the chicken stock and egg noodles. Bake 15 minutes more. Serve hot.

Hope Galloway's Spaghetti & Turkey Meatballs

Philadelphia, Pennsylvania

SERVES 4

Source: Hope Gallow

"Spaghetti and meatballs were a tradition in my household, and my grandmother passed the recipe down two generations," says Hope Galloway. "This is a meal that got the whole family to the table and communicating and catching up. It was filling and tasted great, even the next day. It is and will always be one of my family's favorites." Ms. Galloway has updated this beloved recipe to offer a healthier twist: Instead of ground beef she uses ground turkey.

1 pound ground turkey

1 egg

⅓ cup seasoned or Italian breadcrumbs

¼ cup chopped onion

¼ cup chopped green bell pepper

½ teaspoon seasoning salt

¼ teaspoon black pepper

½ cup vegetable oil

1 16-ounce jar marinara sauce

1 box spaghetti cooked according to package directions

Pass It Down TIP

For an even healthier version, Hope Galloway suggests baking the meatballs in a 350° oven for 30 minutes instead of frying them, and using low sodium spaghetti sauce.

In a large bowl, combine the turkey, egg, breadcrumbs, onions, green bell pepper, seasoning salt, and black pepper. Mix well using your hands and form into golf ball-size meatballs.

Heat the oil in a large deep skillet on medium-high. Add the meatballs and fry until brown on all sides, about 5 minutes.

Heat the marinara sauce in a large saucepan and add the meatballs. Simmer for 15 minutes and serve over spaghetti.

Brother Elijah's Turkey Meatloaf

Shoreview, Minnesota

SERVES 6 TO 8

Alisia Marie Brown was educated formally in the culinary arts at California State University, Long Beach and Johnson and Wales University, Charleston. She is currently pursuing a degree to teach culinary arts so she can share her love of cooking with others. Brown says while she has traveled all over the country working in the best restaurants and with skilled chefs, her biggest cooking lessons have come through two generations of family, including her mother and both of her grandmothers, who, incidentally, all made really great meatloaf. Brown developed her meatloaf recipe for her nephew, Elijah. "It's made from ground turkey, instead of the standard beef because it's leaner," she says.

MEATLOAF

3 large eggs, lightly beaten

kosher sea salt, to taste

pepper, to taste

1 cup extra virgin olive oil

3 tablespoons Dijon mustard

2 tablespoons Worcestershire sauce

2 pounds ground turkey

1 cup celery, finely chopped

½ cup carrot, finely chopped

⅓ cup each of yellow and red peppers, finely chopped

1–2 tablespoons chopped garlic

1 cup ricotta cheese

1 tablespoon fresh Italian parsley, finely chopped

1 teaspoon ground cumin

½ teaspoon smoked paprika

6 large leaves fresh sage, finely chopped, or ½ teaspoon dried sage

1 tablespoon onion powder

½ teaspoon liquid smoke

1–1½ cups Italian bread crumbs

SAUCE (OR GRAVY)

1 cup finely diced onion
1 tablespoon finely chopped garlic
½ teaspoon crushed red pepper
1 teaspoon kosher sea salt or to taste
2 cups orange juice
2 tablespoons Worcestershire sauce
1 teaspoon liquid smoke
½ cup light brown sugar or molasses
1 cup vegetable stock
2–3 tablespoons of tomato paste

Preheat your oven to 350° F. In a small bowl, gently combine the eggs, salt, pepper, olive oil, Dijon mustard, and Worcestershire sauce and whisk together. In a large bowl, combine the turkey and the rest of the ingredients, except the bread crumbs. Add in the mixture from the first bowl and mix.

Fold in your bread crumbs to mixture until well incorporated.

Using a pan spray, coat a sheet pan and form your meat loaf. Once it is formed, place in the refrigerator for 20 minutes to an hour before cooking.

Bake at 350° F for 1 hour covered. Then put sauce on top and bake uncovered for 20 minutes.

FOR SAUCE

Sauté your onion in a heavy pan until golden. Add garlic, crushed red pepper, and salt and allow the garlic to soften.

Add the orange juice. Bring to a boil, and then allow to simmer for 5 minutes. Add the Worcestershire sauce, liquid smoke, brown sugar or molasses, stock, and the tomato paste.

Allow to cook and thicken for 20 minutes. Add more pepper and salt to taste.

Roasted Turkey Wings with Mushroom Gravy

Norfolk, Virginia

SERVES 4 TO 6

Junell Thompson says her mother, June, cooked this simple dish for her and her brother back in the 70s. "I love turkey wings, but turkey drumsticks and breasts go well with this recipe and are prepared the same way," she says. "My mother sometimes made the mushroom gravy from scratch, which is the best way, but here is the simple version for today's busy mothers, which substitutes the scratch gravy with canned mushroom gravy."

4 large turkey wings
3 tablespoons salt
3 tablespoons freshly ground pepper
2 tablespoons dry rosemary
6 tablespoons unsalted butter, thinly sliced
½ cup water
3 bay leaves
1 cup sliced yellow onions
1 14-ounce can mushroom gravy

Preheat the oven to 370° F.

Wash turkey wings off under cold water, pat dry, and set aside. Season the turkey wings with salt, pepper, and dry rosemary. Set aside.

In a large baking dish or roasting pan lined with foil, spread the sliced butter and pour the water in the base of the dish. Arrange the turkey wings, bay leaf, and sliced onions on top.

Cover the baking dish with aluminum foil and place in the oven. Roast, turning the wings every 20 minutes, until the wings are fork tender—about 1 hour.

Remove the pan of turkey wings from oven. Set aside. In a small saucepan, heat can of mushroom gravy to desired temperature, pour over turkey wings, and serve.

··· Presidential Cooks ···

Cooking Truth to Power

BY ADRIAN MILLER

Source: Library of Congress

Adrian Miller is a former special assistant to President William Jefferson Clinton, and a former deputy director of the President's Initiative for One America. He worked in the White House from October 1999 to January 2001. Mr. Miller is currently researching and writing a history of soul food.

Benjamin Harrison, the twenty-third president of the U.S. (1889–1893), had little use for the culinary stylings of the French chef already in residence at the White House when he took office. He called on his longtime family cook, Dolly Johnson, to take over the presidential kitchen because he favored her "plain dishes."

For two centuries, African American cooks have pleased the palates of our presidents. The presidential kitchen has long been a mélange of culinary skill and racial caste. Several American presidents were slave-owning Southerners who transplanted their plantation cooks to the executive kitchen. Beset with high expectations and limited liberty, black cooks consistently displayed their artistry while working, living, and sleeping in the White House kitchen.

Source: Library of Congress

White House Kitchen 1907—African American cooks consistently comprised the majority of kitchen workers in the executive mansion, well into the 1960s.

Antebellum presidents also regularly hired classically trained chefs and outside caterers—both free African Americans and Europeans—to cook their meals, particularly when entertaining guests. Mirroring American society at large, the diversity of the White House's culinary staff created an interesting, though complicated, racial dynamic.

European chefs catered to elite tastes with continental cuisine. These aristocratic dishes graced the table for lavish public affairs, such as inaugural balls and state dinners. Presidents have also retained their own private chefs, many of them African American, to make daily meals for the First Family and entertain guests at smaller affairs. These home-cooked meals featured a variety of regional American specialties, particularly from the American South. As a result, haute cuisine and home cooking thrived side by side, and even rivaled each other, in the White House kitchen.

Haute cuisine often carried more social prestige and captured the public's imagination, but several presidents have confessed that it was the comfort food of their black cooks that they preferred and praised. George Washington savored the peas, hoe cakes, and fish expertly prepared by Samuel Fraunces, his free West Indian steward. Eddy and Fanny, two enslaved women, regularly ignored the dictates of Jefferson's French chef and made sure the president got his black-eyed peas, okra, and sweet potatoes the way he liked them.

According to the memoirs of Alonzo Fields, a long-time White House butler, even the aristocratic Franklin Delano Roosevelt relished some homey touches. FDR and Winston Churchill once dined on sweet-and-sour pigs' feet at a private luncheon. FDR got the recipe from Norway's Princess Martha, but it was probably prepared by a member of the White House's all-black culinary staff: Ida Allen (chief cook), Catherine Smith, Elizabeth Moore, and Elizabeth Blake.[20]

Yet the prestige of cooking for a president was not enough when liberty was out of reach. Enslaved cooks yearned for freedom, and sometimes they got it. Hercules, George Washington's enslaved cook, disappeared with his son in March 1797 just as President Washington was ending his second term and retiring to Mount Vernon, Virginia. Evidencing her dependence on Hercules, a vexed Martha Washington penned a letter to her sister that said: "[I] am obliged to be my one (sic) Housekeeper which takes up the greatest part of my time,—our cook Hercules went away so that I am as much at a loss for a cook as for a house keeper.—altogether I am sadly plaiged [sic]."

Once formal freedom was secured for African Americans, from Emancipation until the present day, black cooks in the White House have practiced their culinary craft on their own terms. Some got the cook's job due to a prior stint as a family servant. Shortly after moving into the White House, President William and Mrs. McKinley fired President Cleveland's cook and hired the African American man who cooked for them in Canton, Ohio. The McKinleys believed that "never was anyone equal to him, and in preparing beefsteak and onions, the favorite dish of the President, he has attained perfection."[21]

Hercules, President George Washington's enslaved cook.

President Benjamin Harrison garnered national headlines when he hired Dolly Johnson, a Kentucky cook, who prepared his meals while he lived in Indianapolis. She quickly made everyone forget about the French cooking of her predecessor, Madame Marcel Pelonard. Johnson's obituary noted that she was "famous throughout the South for her culinary skill."[22]

Others were recruited as professional cooks. Alice Howard came to the White House staff in the early 1900s and served as the assistant cook for three very different presidents. Theodore Roosevelt and Woodrow Wilson were united on little else than their love for her corn pone,[23] while William Howard Taft craved her fried chicken.[24]

Zephyr Wright, the White House's last true family cook, served Lyndon Baines Johnson for decades, and they shared a special bond. Zephyr Wright's life experiences under Jim Crow motivated Johnson to push for landmark civil rights legislation as a U.S. senator, as vice president, and then as president of the United States. LBJ once asked Mrs. Wright to drive back to Texas from Washington, DC. She flatly refused, describing the indignities that she had to suffer of being denied access to food, lodging, and even a bathroom while traveling through Southern states.

LBJ took note and told her story to anyone who would listen—and those who would not. Harry McPherson, a former Johnson aide, remembered one such encounter when then Vice President Johnson pressed his case to an unsympathetic Mississippi Senator John Stennis on the floor of the U.S. Senate.[25] Johnson ultimately acknowledged his debt. When he signed the Civil Rights Act of 1964, he presented the pen he used to Zephyr Wright, saying, "You deserve this more than anyone else."[26]

Johnson also crowed about Mrs. Wright's chili and peach ice cream. Just the mention of her chili caused a national sensation. Ladybird Johnson said that requests for the recipe were "almost as popular as the government pamphlet on the care and feeding of children."[27] Once, Mrs. Wright made an elegant beef hash for a private lunch that President Johnson had with former president Harry Truman and Frank Dobie, a well-known Texas folklorist. Dobie said it was the best he had ever eaten and wrote Mrs. Wright for the recipe.[28]

Unsurprisingly, our presidents often celebrated the food because it gave them great comfort. President Jefferson probably said it best when he penned a letter from the White House in November 1802 to his daughter at Monticello seeking the enslaved Peter Hemings's recipe for English muffins: "Pray enable yourself to direct us here how to make muffins in Peter's method. My cook here cannot succeed at all in them, and they are *a great luxury to me* (emphasis added)."[29]

Samuel Fraunces' Beef Brazilian Onions

New York, New York

SERVES 8

Samuel Fraunces, a free man of West Indian heritage, was a well-known and highly regarded tavern owner in New York City during the American Revolution. During that time, George Washington was a frequent customer of his, and he served him a dish called "onions done in the Brazilian way." It was one of several delicacies that pleased Washington, and he hired Fraunces to be his steward once Washington became president. Adrian Miller, an African American historian and student of black presidential chefs, has adapted this recipe to be lighter by swapping out the onions, eggs, and butter in the original recipe for sweet onion, egg whites, and olive oil. For more adventurous cooks, Miller offers the option of substituting bison meat for beef. Either way, this recipe is delicious enough to please any president.

ONIONS

4 medium-size sweet onions (e.g., Vidalia, Walla Walla, or Maui Sweets)
4 egg whites beaten with 1 tablespoon of water
¼ cup of olive oil

BEEF MINCEMEAT MIXTURE

½ pound of ground beef or bison
1 green bell pepper, chopped
1 garlic clove, minced
¼ cup beef stock
¼ teaspoon dried sage
¼ teaspoon dried oregano
salt and pepper to taste

Where do you find bison? Look no further—Eatwild is the most comprehensive source for grass-fed meat and dairy products in the United States and Canada; lists more than 1,100 pasture-based farms that produce beef, lamb, pork, bison, and other meats. Visit them at www.eatwild.com.

Peel the onions, cut in half, and set aside.

Bring large pot of water to a boil and add the onions. Parboil them for 5 minutes. Remove and cool.

When cool enough to handle, remove the inner core of the onion to create a "cup." Set the "cups" aside.

Prepare the bison meat mixture by combining all the ingredients.

Fill the onion cups with bison meat mixture and pack it in just enough so that the mixture doesn't fall out.

Glaze the top of the stuffed onions with the egg white wash.

Heat the olive oil in a large fry pan over medium heat. Carefully place the onions, meat side down onto the hot fry pan. Fry for 5 minutes or until the meat mixture is cooked thoroughly.

Serve as an appetizer, stuffing side up.

Source: Library of Congress

Well into the 20th century, even as the adoption and enforcement of laws of equality eluded the senators they cooked for, the Senate cooks demonstrated skill and prowess with both complex and everyday dishes to tempt lawmakers' palates.

Beef Turnip Stew with Rice

Hempstead, Texas

SERVES 4

Margo Gillum grew up in deep south Louisiana, about 50 miles west of New Orleans. Her mother was always looking to stretch a dime and a meal. Plentiful turnips or cabbage were filling and cheap, but Ms. Gillum and her six siblings didn't care for them much. "To get us to eat them, she would add them to any type of beef, mostly beef neck bones and stew meat," she says. "The goal of the recipe was to change the taste of the turnips and it worked." Today, Ms. Gillum says she loves turnips, ranking them as one of her top comfort foods thanks to her mom, Rebecca, down in Thibodaux, Louisiana.

¼ cup canola oil
1 pound beef stew meat or beef neck bones
4 tablespoons flour
1 large onion, chopped
⅛ cup chopped bell pepper
2 garlic cloves, minced
3 cups water or beef stock (page 11)
5 medium to large turnips, cut into quarters
1 teaspoon garlic powder
salt and pepper to taste

Heat the canola oil over medium-high heat in a deep, heavy pot.

Add the beef and brown on all sides, about 3 to 4 minutes. Remove from the pot.

Pour canola in pot, brown beef, and remove from pot. Set aside.

Add the flour to the same oil in which you browned the beef. Cook, stirring constantly with a wooden spoon, until the mixture (roux) becomes brown, about 3 minutes.

Add the onion, bell pepper, and garlic. Cook for 2–3 minutes, always stirring, and return browned beef to the pot. Stir in the beef stock and simmer over low-medium heat for 40 minutes or until the beef is tender.

Add the turnips to the pot along with garlic powder, salt, and pepper to taste. Simmer 15 minutes more or until turnips are tender. Serve over rice or with cornbread.

Chef Jeff's Slow-Braised Oxtails with Steamed White Rice

Las Vegas, Nevada

SERVES 4 TO 6

"Oxtails. I love them, love them, love them," says Chef Jeff. "Slow cooked in beef broth with aromatic vegetables and fresh herbs, these tender pieces of meat on the bone will stand up against any cut of beef. I did not grow up eating oxtails. I was introduced to them some 20 years ago and I can tell you, they are best served with steamed white rice, braised cabbage, and sweet cornbread. Keep that natural broth, strain it, and let it cook down, then spoon it over oxtails and rice."

3½ pounds oxtails, cleaned and fat trimmed
1½ tablespoons fresh ground black pepper
2 tablespoons kosher salt
2 tablespoons vegetable oil
1 tablespoon fresh garlic, minced
½ cup yellow onions, small diced
½ cup green bell peppers, small diced
2 bay leaves
4 cups beef broth

Rinse off oxtails, season with salt and pepper, set aside.

In a medium stockpot, add vegetable oil over medium heat.

When oil is hot but not smoking, add oxtails to pot and brown on all sides.

Add garlic, onions, bell peppers, and bay leaf. Stir all ingredients for 2 minutes.

Add beef broth, reduce heat to a very low simmer, and let cook for 4½ hours or until meat is tender and falling off the bone.

Spicy Steak & Mac

Okolona, Mississippi

SERVES 4 TO 6

Despite cooking for a "long, long time," Teresa Fields says that cooking remains a major source of enjoyment. She considers her ability to cook things folks love a gift from above. "I just give it to the good Lord above that he allowed me to have this gift," says Ms. Fields. "It's all about making food fun and bringing family and friends together." This perfectly easy one-pot meal will bring folks quickly around the table to enjoy the tenderness of the steak and the comforting creaminess of the macaroni and cheese.

2 pounds tender beef (such as tenderloin, London Broil, or other tender beef cut; or 2 pounds chicken breast, sliced)
3 tablespoons butter
1 yellow onion, chopped
2 cloves garlic, minced
1¼ tablespoons cayenne pepper
2¼ tablespoons minced parsley
3 cups macaroni noodles
3 cups shredded Monterey Jack cheese, or cheese of your choice
salt and pepper to taste

Place the beef or chicken in a wide, deep skillet with 3 cups of water. Bring to a simmer and cover. Cook 15 minutes or until the meat is cooked through and tender.

Remove the lid and add the butter, onion, garlic, cayenne pepper, and parsley. Mix well and add the noodles. Cover and cook 5–7 minutes or until noodles are tender.

Stir in the shredded cheese and salt and pepper to taste. Simmer, uncovered, for 2–3 minutes or until the mixture is thickened slightly and not watery.

··· The Black Hunter ···

Source: Library of Congress

Courtesy: Born in Slavery: Slave Narratives from the Federal Writers'
Project, 1936–1938, Library of Congress American Memory Collection

During slavery and later during post-Emancipation subsistence farming, African Americans had little access to quality cuts of meat. Often protein came from the offal, or "garbage cuts" of slaughtered livestock that plantation owners would not allow to grace their tables. These included everything from organ meats to trotters, snouts, and tails. Because of this, hunting wild game and fishing was a way to put meat on the table in the form of venison, opossum, raccoon, squirrel, turtle, and rabbit.

As Frederick Douglass Opie writes in Hog and Hominy: Soul Food from Africa to America *(Columbia University Press, 2008), these animals remained staples for rural blacks very much into the 1950s. Besides being plentiful, wild meat served another valuable purpose: Its relative toughness meant it could afford to simmer for long periods of time while a family tended the fields, finally returning to a hot and ready meal at home.*

"I was born in Huntsville County, Alabama . . . in 1850 . . . [As a child] all the work I ever done was pick up chips [manure] for my grandma to cook with. I was kept busy doing this all day. The big boys went out and got rabbits, possums, and fish. I would sho lak to be in old Alabama fishing, 'cause I'm a fisherman. There is sho some pretty water in Alabama and as swift as the cars run here. Water so clear and blue you can see the fish way down and dey wouldn't bite to save your life."

— **Ex-Slave Stephen McCray, 88 years old,
Oklahoma City, Oklahoma, 1937**

Stuffed Quail with Cranberry Glaze

Atlanta, Georgia

SERVES 1

Quail is a small bird that has sweet, tender, and juicy dark meat. Chef Joel Rickerson says he receives rave reviews for his stuffed quail. It's tasty and a welcome change from the traditional stuffed turkey or chicken.

½ tablespoon chopped garlic
2 tablespoons chopped onions
3 tablespoons olive oil
1 cup wild rice
2 cups chicken stock
1 quail
½ cup cranberries
½ cup red wine
½ cup granulated sugar
salt and pepper to taste

Preheat oven to 350° F.

In a small pot over medium heat, add olive oil. Sauté garlic and onions until tender.

Add 1 cup wild rice and 2 cups chicken stock. Cook over medium heat until rice is tender. Once wild rice is tender, allow it to cool down for 15 minutes and then stuff it into the boneless quail. Season well with salt and pepper and place into a small, lightly oiled pan. Cook for 18–20 minutes in the oven at 350° F.

To make the glaze, place cranberries into a small pan and add red wine. Add granulated sugar and cook for 15 minutes. Put cranberry glaze on plate and place quail on top.

PIGS & PORK

Did You Know? *The first pigs came to the New World aboard one of Christopher Colum-bus's ships, which landed in the Caribbean. Later, the explorer Hernando de Soto came to Florida with 13 pigs aboard his ship, and soon enough their numbers grew into the thousands.*

Pigs were an easy source of meat in the colonies because they were easy to raise and provided plenty of flesh. Used for fresh cuts as well as cured meats like salt pork, they were often the most plentiful livestock on any farm. Of course, farms were most often worked by slaves, for whom only the throwaway parts of the pig were available. These included feet, ears, snouts, and organ meats. African Americans found ways to use it all, from stuffing intestines for chitlins (chitterlings) to using a bit of salt, smoked pork, or pork rind to add flavor to what they could grow in their small kitchen garden. Even after slavery ended, particularly in the Jim Crow South, subsistence farming by sharecroppers provided little more by way of either freedom or food, and the skills learned in the bad old plantations days served them well.

Today, pork is a mainstay of soul food—although not the healthiest one because of its high fat content—especially when using the lesser quality cuts that are often most affordable. Consider substituting smoked turkey or turkey bacon in greens or rice dishes that normally call for pork—and save the pork for special occasions when a little extra indulgence is on the menu.

North Carolina Style Ham Hocks

Harlem, New York

SERVES 6 TO 8

Source: Grant H. Reid

Ms. Fannie Pennington was ninety-five years old when she submitted this recipe. It first appeared in Food for the Soul, Recipes from Harlem's Abyssinian Baptist Church *(Random House) where she is a devoted member. "I'm nearly ninety now," she wrote when the book was first published in 2005, "so I don't cook very often. But if I want ham hocks, I know how to make them. I always make them in my iron pot. This recipe came from my mama, Hattie, who was born and raised in rural Macon, North Carolina. She married Papa and moved up north to New York with him. Mama always served this with hot cornbread (see Sylvia's Spoon Bread recipe, page 50) and butter. Papa loved her ham hocks, and so did the rest of our family. Papa would always say, 'Make sure to drink that juice. It's good for you. That is pot-lickin' juice.'"*

4 smoked ham hocks
2 slices salt pork
1 medium onion, chopped
2 garlic cloves, minced
2 bunches kale, stalks off
1 red bell pepper, cored, seeded, and quartered
4 small white turnips, quartered
black pepper

Place ham hocks and salt pork in a pot with 8 quarts of water and bring to a boil over high heat.

Remove the salt pork when broth is salty enough for your taste.

Add the onion and garlic and boil for 1½ hours or until they are tender.

Add the kale, red pepper, and turnips. Season with pepper to taste, and simmer until kale is tender. The total cooking time will be about 2–2½ hours.

Anita Dawkins's Pork & Sauerkraut

Lithonia, Georgia

SERVES 4

Source: Anita Dawkins

Anita Dawkins makes this dish every New Year's Day. Its comforting simplicity makes it ideal for any winter's day. She serves it over homemade mashed potatoes on her overflowing New Year's dinner table.

1 4-pound center-cut bone-in pork loin (rib) roast
¼ teaspoon salt
½ teaspoon black pepper
¼ cup vegetable shortening
1 cup water
1 large onion, sliced
1-pound bag or jar of sauerkraut

Pass It Down TIP

Vegetable shortenings are high in trans fats. Substitute canola oil for a heart-healthy omega acid-rich substitute.

Preheat oven to 350° F. Sprinkle the pork with the salt and half the pepper. Set aside.

Melt the vegetable shortening or oil (see tip below) in a large skillet over medium-high heat. Add the pork loin and sear on all sides until golden brown, about 7–10 minutes per side.

Remove the pork loin from the skillet and place it in a roasting pan or Dutch oven. Add the pan drippings from the skillet to the roasting pan with the water, onion, sauerkraut, and remaining pepper.

Cover and bake for two hours or until pork is fork tender. Serve with mashed potatoes.

Donna Daniels' Pork Chops with Shallots, Lemon, and Capers

Guilford, Connecticut

SERVES 4

Perhaps because of her parents' Southern roots or the affordability of pork chops, Donna Daniels says her family ate pork chops once a week while she was growing up in Philadelphia. "I'm sure the fact that they were relatively quick and easy to cook would have been a help to my mother, who was a very busy and dedicated public school teacher. Her preparation was simple: The chops were seasoned with salt and pepper, pan fried, and then smothered. Her pan drippings were the best and she often served her chops with rice, a perfect conductor for the drippings." Dr. Daniels' recipe builds on her mother's and uses tricks she learned from cookbook author Mark Bittman. "I learned from his suggestions and innovated on my mother's approach while using some flavors that I love: Marash chile flakes, shallots, and capers," she says. "I see this recipe as an extension of my mother's, a tribute really, but with a touch of her daughter's curiosity about other cuisines."

4 center-cut loin pork chops, bone-in, about 1 inch thick
kosher salt
freshly ground black pepper
2 teaspoons Marash chile flakes (available in Middle Eastern markets) or paprika
4 tablespoons olive oil
½ cup dry white wine
1 teaspoon minced garlic
4 tablespoons minced shallots
½ cup chicken or vegetable stock
1 heaping tablespoon capers
1 tablespoon sweet butter
1 tablespoon freshly squeezed lemon juice
4–5 tablespoons finely chopped flat-leaf parsley for garnish

Season chops with salt, pepper, and Marash chile flakes.

In a small skillet, add 1 tablespoon of the olive oil and heat on medium-high heat for 1 minute. Add the garlic, cook 45 seconds to 1 minute, then add the shallots and sauté another 2 minutes. Remove from heat and set aside.

Heat a large skillet over medium-high heat for 2–3 minutes. Add the remaining 3 tablespoons of olive oil and heat 30 seconds. Add the pork chops and raise heat to high. Brown chops on both sides, moving them around so they develop good color all over, no longer than 4 minutes total.

Reduce heat to medium. Add the wine, garlic, and shallot mixture to pork chops. Cook, turning the chops once or twice, until the wine is evaporated, about 3 minutes. Add the stock, turn the heat down to low, cover, and cook for 10–12 minutes, turning chops once or twice. Add capers and cook another 2–3 minutes until chops are tender but not dry. When done, they'll be firm to the touch.

Transfer the pork chops to a platter. If the pan juices are very thin, continue to cook them, stirring and scraping the bottom of the pan until the liquid is reduced slightly. Stir in the butter and lemon juice, pour over chops, garnish with parsley, and serve with rice or baked potatoes.

Peach-Glazed Easter Ham

Olathe, Kansas

SERVES 10 TO 12

Renea Feagin is a dedicated wife and mother who loves to cook and bake. A self-taught cook who says she is at her most creative in the kitchen preparing meals for her three kids and two grandkids, Ms. Feagin's Peach-Glazed Easter Ham recipe originally came from her friend Annie—and then she added her own twists. "The final result was a hit with my husband at our 2005 Thanksgiving dinner," she says. "No more waiting in line at those expensive ham stores the day before Easter or Christmas. This recipe is a keeper and is sure to be passed down from generation to generation."

2 tablespoons whole cloves

2 cups packed brown sugar

1 stick butter

¼ cup orange juice

1 16-ounce can peaches with the juice

¼ cup spicy brown mustard

½ cup peach or apricot preserves

1 teaspoon cinnamon

2 teaspoons allspice

1 teaspoon ginger

1 10–14-pound precooked ham

1 large plastic marinating bag with twist tie

Pass It Down TIP

Renea Feagin says you kick this recipe up a notch or two by adding 2 tablespoons of peach liqueur, such as schnapps, to the peach glaze before baking.

Mix 1 tablespoon of the cloves with brown sugar, butter, orange juice, liquid from peaches, mustard, preserves, cinnamon, allspice, and ginger together in a large saucepan. Cook on medium heat until mixture becomes thick and bubbly. Remove from heat and let cool.

Rinse ham and pat dry. Press the remaining cloves evenly all over the ham. Place ham in the plastic roasting bag and pour the cooled peach glaze over ham. The glaze will be very thick.

Close the bag tightly with twist tie and leave the ham in refrigerator overnight. Next day, remove it from the refrigerator and put peaches on top, securing with toothpicks. Place ham on cooking rack and put in a baking pan. Pour the glaze from the marinating bag all over ham.

Cover the ham tightly with foil and place in a preheated 325° F oven. Bake 18 minutes per pound. Cook the ham 1–1½ hours covered, then remove the foil and finish cooking. Baste ham with the pan drippings every 20 minutes.

Dwight Jones' St. Louis-Style Spareribs

St. Louis, Missouri

Dwight Jones was born in Hayti, Missouri, the son of a teacher and the town barber shop owner. In many ways, his upbringing reflected a traditional African American experience. His was a small town where folks knew each other. Men would pass the time of day at his dad's barbershop. His parents kept a large garden plot every summer from which meals were prepared, just as their parents and grandparents did before them. After high school, Mr. Jones went to college to become an engineer for Boeing Aerospace in St. Louis. His work has brought him to every corner of the world, and where his work doesn't take him, his passion for game fishing and hunting does. Most of all, Mr. Jones loves to cook—so much so he traveled to New York City every weekend for an entire year to complete a professional chef's certificate at the Institute for Culinary Education, all the while holding down his demanding full-time job. But the thing that Mr. Jones is most known for is his skill with a smoker. Come any day the weather is fine, you'll find him and some pals smoking racks of ribs on a specially made smoker, complete with a rig for towing behind his truck.

3 racks St. Louis-style pork ribs (about 8 pounds)
1 cup BBQ Spice Blend

BBQ SPICE RUB BLEND

2½ ounces coarse salt
2 ounces granulated garlic
2 ounces onion powder
⅔ ounce dry mustard
½ ounce red pepper
⅓ ounce black pepper
2½ ounces paprika
½ ounce dried thyme leaves

Pass It Down TIP

For a healthful and delicious veggie barbecue, toss sliced fresh vegetables, like zucchini, squash, peppers, and eggplant, with a dash of olive oil and enough Spice Rub Blend to coat. Grill 10-15 minutes or until vegetables are fork tender but not mushy.

Mix together and save in a sealable glass jar.

Coat the ribs evenly with the spice blend and let rest in the refrigerator for at least 2 hours or overnight.

Heat your grill to 350° F. if using gas, or until coals are red hot if using briquettes or hardwood charcoal.

Place the ribs in the grill away from the coals or direct flame. If using charcoal, you may spray the coals lightly with cold water to prevent them from getting too hot, as needed. Cover the grill, cook slowly for approximately 4 hours, turning every 30 minutes. The internal temperature should be at 170° F. The ribs should be well crusted on both sides.

Although Dwight Jones developed this rub for his St. Louis Style Spareribs (page 91), it works wonderfully on wings, chicken, and anything that can be grilled. Keeps for up to two months when stored in a cool dry place. Serve with your favorite BBQ sauce and other side dishes.

Russel Honoré's Barbecued Boston Pork Butt

Baton Rouge, Louisiana

SERVES 8 TO 10

Source: Robert Carr

Lieutenant General Russel Honoré (retired) leaves most of the cooking to his wife, Beverly, but he is master of his own grill and, he says, he grills year-round regardless of the weather. His Barbecued Boston Pork Butt is favored by his family as a high calorie wind-up to the long Thanksgiving weekend. His special seasoning mix is so beloved by family and friends that he's often pressed to share the recipe. Answering the call of duty, the general has teamed up with famed New Orleans chef Paul Prudhomme to create Honore's Spice blends, including a low-sodium version that will be available in the New Orleans area and online.

1 10-pound Boston butt
4 tablespoons salt
4 tablespoons black pepper
4 tablespoons paprika
4 tablespoons garlic powder
4 garlic cloves
4 whole cayenne peppers

Pass It Down TIP

You can do this recipe without the use of a grill, by browning the roast on all sides in a large fry pan, or even in the same Dutch oven in which you'll complete the cooking.

Preheat oven to 325° F.

In a small bowl, mix together salt, pepper, paprika, and garlic powder, and work the mixture into the meat. With a sharp knife, make four holes in the roast and plug each hole with a garlic clove and a whole red cayenne pepper.

Heat grill (charcoal or gas) on high. Put roast on grill and sear on each side until butt is browned but not burned, about 20 minutes per side. Stay with the grill to ensure the roast does not scorch. If using a charcoal grill or smoker, you may add your favorite wood chips to the fire if you like the smoke flavor.

Remove roast from grill and put into covered Dutch oven or any roaster covered with aluminum foil. Roast in oven for a half hour, then reduce heat to 280° F and roast for another 2½ hours or about 15 minutes per pound, until the roast registers an internal temperature of 170°.

Remove from oven when cooked and let stand for 15 minutes before slicing. You should have a lot of gravy in pan. Skim off grease from pan gravy and serve roast with a plate of white beans and rice, or on crusty bread with pan juices.

CHAPTER

4

Seafood

Pass It Down Classic Louisiana Crawfish Boil**

Louisiana

SERVES 4

Source: Library of Congress

Crawfish are plentiful in Louisiana and are a popular casual feast dish. The name crawfish boil is misleading because it's not just crawfish that goes in the pot, but potatoes, corn, and even sausage—if it's not Lent. Boiling crawfish calls for some pretty big pots and a big enough stove or fire to do it right, which is why most people go out for theirs. Anybody in Louisiana will tell you—no matter their color, station, or class— that the best way to eat boiled crawfish is from a big old pile set down on newspaper at a picnic table!

20 pounds crawfish
10 gallons water
1 cup salt
12 small red potatoes
1 head garlic, cloves peeled and smashed slightly
5 small yellow onions, peeled
1 tablespoon cayenne pepper, or more to taste
3 lemons, cut in half
4 ears corn, cut in half
2 andouille sausage cut in half

Place all the ingredients in a 60-quart stockpot, or divide them equally between two 30-quart stockpots.

Bring to a boil and simmer for 15 minutes.

Cover the pot, remove the heat, and allow the crawfish boil to steep 15–20 minutes longer.

Strain out the corn and potatoes and place them on a platter. Strain out the crawfish and put them on a newspaper-lined picnic table to pick apart and enjoy.

** Recipe adapted from Louisiana Crawfish Recipes by the Louisiana Department of Agriculture

HOW TO EAT BOILED CRAWFISH

The biggest part of the fun in a crawfish boil is the ritual of getting to the meat. Messy as it is, you'll find folks high and low camped out at picnic tables, twisting off the heads and pulling out the tail for the sweet succulent meat. Here's how to do it:

1. Hold the front of the crawfish in one hand, and use your other hand to grab just above the tail.

2. Twist the body so that the tail separates from the head.

3. Suck on the head to get all the cooking juices—traditional but optional!

4. Grasp the tail tightly and pull out the meat inside. Gobble it up and enjoy!

Did You Know? *Although they may look like shrimp, crawfish, or "crayfish" as they're called in the North, are freshwater crustaceans that live in grassy, deep wetlands, where the water doesn't freeze.*

Pass It Down TIP

The generally accepted rule of thumb for figuring out how much crawfish to throw in the pot is 5 pounds per person, along with 1 ear of corn and 1 or 2 small potatoes. Of course, if your folks have a bigger appetite, feel free to throw in more. Odds are they'll sure enough be eaten. Use 1 gallon of water for every 2 pounds of crawfish you're boiling.

Crawfish Étouffée

New Orleans, Louisiana

SERVES 4 TO 6

Justin Gaines, a chef in New Jersey, spent half a year training in New Orleans after he left the CIA. "While I was there, for months I was not allowed to make jambalaya, gumbo, étouffée, or even shrimp Creole because I wasn't born there. I just had to watch." Eventually, he got his chance and quickly mastered all the Cajun and Creole dishes, like this crawfish étouffée.

½ cup olive oil or vegetable oil

2 links of half-cooked andouille sausage, chopped small

1 green bell pepper, chopped small

2 stalks of celery, chopped small

1 medium red onion, chopped small

½ teaspoon salt or to taste

¼ teaspoon black pepper or to taste

3 teaspoons Creole seasoning (page 233)

1 tablespoon chopped garlic

½ cup of cup dry sherry

¼ cup white wine (Chardonnay)

1¼ cups tomato sauce

¾ cup canola oil

1 cup of flour

3 quarts of crawfish stock (hot)

½ pound of shrimp, cleaned and chopped

1 pound of crawfish tails

1 tomato, peeled and seeded

¼ cup heavy cream

½ stick unsalted butter

dash of hot sauce

Crawfish, shrimp, or other shellfish stock is easy and quick to prepare. Just add 1 cup of heads and peelings to 2 cups of boiling water and simmer for 30 minutes. Strain and use. You can increase the volume at the same ratio.

In a stockpot, sauté diced andouille in olive oil, brown lightly. Add all vegetables except tomatoes, sweat and season with salt, black pepper, and Creole seasoning for 5–7 minutes.

Add chopped garlic, raise heat to medium-high, cook for 2 minutes, and add the sherry. Cook until sherry is almost totally evaporated and add the white wine. Cook until the wine is almost totally evaporated and add the tomato sauce.

In another medium saucepan, heat the canola oil and whisk in the flour. Stir with a wooden spoon to make a light roux, 5–10 minutes.

Add the roux to the stockpot. Add the crawfish stock in thirds and whisk well to break up any lumps. Season with Creole seasoning.

Bring the mixture to a boil. Drop to a simmer for about 45 minutes, or until the mixture is thick enough to coat the back of a spoon.

Season with Creole seasoning and adjust salt and pepper to taste. Add shrimp, crawfish, chopped tomatoes, cream, butter, and a dash of hot sauce to finish. Cool completely and refrigerate overnight. Serve reheated the next day with steamed rice.

Pass It Down TIP

To peel and seed a tomato—also called tomato concassé—use a sharp paring knife. Score the tomato on the bottom in an X. Have a bowl ready with 1 cup of ice and 1 cup of water. Bring a pot of water to a boil and drop the tomato in for 30 seconds, then drop it in the ice water. Remove the tomato from the water after 15 seconds and the skin will peel away easily. Slice in half and gently remove seeds with a spoon. Chop as desired.

Love Letter Shrimp & Grits

Warwick, Rhode Island

SERVES 4

Source: Robin Frye

Robyn Frye counts herself as "one who God has smiled on," overcoming 18 years of addiction and multiple jail stints. In addition to hoping she is an example to others that someone can come back from life on the edge, one of the other ways she loves to give back in gratitude for getting her life on track is to cook dishes like her Love Letter Shrimp for family and friends.

2 pounds jumbo shrimp, shelled and deveined
½ cup shredded mozzarella cheese
1 pound thick-cut bacon
1 teaspoon Old Bay Seafood Seasoning
½ cup Antebellum Barbecue Sauce (page 235) or your favorite sauce
chopped parsley for garnish (optional)

Preheat oven to broil.

Using a small knife, slice the shrimp along its underside so that it opens out like a butterfly. Do not slice all the way through.

Take 1 tablespoon of the shredded mozzarella and place it inside the shrimp.

Wrap the stuffed shrimp with a slice of bacon. Insert a wooden skewer from the tail of shrimp through to the top meaty part. Your shrimp should look like the letter "C" on the skewer. Continue this process until the skewers are full.

Add the Old Bay Seasoning to the barbecue sauce and stir well. Brush the skewered shrimp with the barbeque sauce mixture.

Spray the broiling pan lightly with cooking spray or rub with a leftover piece of bacon so it's well greased. Place shrimp in oven and broil until the bacon wrapping is crisp, about 15 minutes. Watch carefully to ensure the shrimp do not burn.

Remove the shrimp and allow to cool for 10 minutes.

Serve the shrimp over a bowl of grits (page 176) and garnish with chopped parsley.

Pass It Down Classic Variation: Charleston Style Shrimp & Grits

SERVES 4

Shrimp and grits is a dish now associated with Charleston, South Carolina, but before it hit the restaurant scene it was a simple everyday dish among the low country people who made good use of what was plentiful in the waters and lands that surrounded them. No one had more creative and delicious ways to prepare this bounty than the Gullah/Geechee people. Here is a version of the classic shrimp and grits that was and is often prepared in Gullah/Geechee homes.

4 slices of thick-cut bacon, chopped
1½ pounds shrimp, peeled and cleaned
3 scallions, minced
1 tablespoon, minced parsley
1 clove garlic, minced
1 large, ripe tomato, chopped
½ teaspoon Creole seasoning (page 233)
⅛ teaspoon cayenne pepper or 2 dashes of Tabasco sauce, or to taste
salt and freshly ground pepper to taste

Heat a large fry pan and add the bacon. Fry until cooked well, but not crispy. Remove with a slotted spoon and drain all but about 2 teaspoons of the bacon grease.

Add the shrimp and scallions, and stir well. Just as shrimp begins to turn pink add the parsley and garlic. Cook for 30 seconds and then add the tomatoes and cook 1 minute more.

Stir in the Creole spice mixture, cayenne, or Tabasco and salt and pepper to taste.

Serve over grits.

Source: Library of Congress

African Americans remained integral to all aspects of food production throughout America long after slavery was abolished. In areas that were rich in oysters and clams, African Americans did most of the harvesting and shucking. Just as in food advertising, their hard-labor contributions were often the source of entertainment and humor for white society.

Did You Know? *This lyric sheet from 1905 depicts a stereotypical "cheerful" black oysterman as an Uncle Remus character working tongs on a boat in the Chesapeake Bay, an area world-renowned for its oysters at that time. The song tells the tale of a lackadaisical fisherman who enjoys lazy days on the water, digging and hauling oysters by hand, untroubled by the faster, steel skipjack boats that harvested oysters by dredging, effectively putting hand-harvesters out of business. Today, the Chesapeake Bay oyster industry is practically non-existent because of overfishing and other adverse environmental impacts.*

The song and imagery in this advertisement touches, although perhaps unintentionally, on an important progression in American history: the advent of food production technology casting aside the important heritage of manual laborers, who were very often African American and whose methods usually created lower environmental impacts on the land and water—methods that are being re-examined and re-implemented today to try and save overused resources before it is too late.

New Orleans Style Friday Fish Fry

Los Angeles, California

SERVES 4 TO 6

"New Orleans Style 'Friday Fish Fry' was my granddaddy's way to bring family together every Friday night," says Chef Jeff. "Grandaddy was an amazing cook who prepared all the family meals. Though Granddaddy never wrote down recipes, he had no problem letting folks come in the kitchen to see what was going down. He used the same seasonings and cornmeal for all three seafoods. I love my granddaddy Charles and grandmother Ethel Mae—this recipe is a special tribute to them. They taught all of us a little something about Southern cooking and life in their own way. May God bless their souls."

4 cups canola oil

14 large Louisiana oysters, shucked

14 jumbo shrimp, peeled, split, and cleaned

4 pieces of red snapper skinless filet, 4 to 6 ounces each

kosher salt and freshly ground pepper

4 large eggs

⅓ cup buttermilk

1 cup ground cornmeal

1 cup all-purpose flour

1 tablespoon cayenne pepper

10 tablespoons onion powder

5 large russet potatoes, peeled, washed, and thinly sliced

Pass It Down TIP

The Friday Fish Fry is best served right out of the grease with garden salad, coleslaw, potato salad, or fresh corn on the cob.

In a deep-fryer or a large cast iron skillet, heat the oil to about 350° F. Test the heat of the oil with a piece of shrimp. If it begins to fry without the oil bubbling and popping, the oil is hot and ready.

On a plate lined with paper towels or a brown paper bag, season all the seafood lightly with salt and pepper. Set aside.

Add the eggs and buttermilk to a large bowl and whisk thoroughly together. Season each with a pinch of salt and pepper. Add all the seasoned seafood to the egg mixture and coat well.

Mix the cornmeal, flour, and all the spices together in a large bowl. Add the buttermilk-marinated seafood to the cornmeal mixture in batches. Coat well.

Using a pair of tongs, drop the cornmeal-breaded seafood into the oil in small batches. Deep-fry until cooked thoroughly and crispy, about 8–10 minutes. Remove and drain on a plate lined with paper towels.

Marinate the thinly sliced potatoes wedges in the buttermilk mixture, then in the cornmeal mixture. Fry until golden brown, about 12–15 minutes. Remove and drain on a plate lined with paper towels.

Charles & Ethel Henderson

Source: Jeff Henderson

Four State Oyster Dressing

Beverly Hills, California

SERVES 6 TO 8

Source: Sherrie Burrell

Public relations and marketing consultant Sherrie Darnise Burrell shares this oyster dressing that she created from two family recipes—one from her parents, Thelma and Columbus Burrell, and another from her godmother, Patricia A. Lynch. "It is one of our family's main holiday dishes and can be found in my memoir, My Mother's Cookbook," says Burrell.

2 tablespoons butter

1 large onion, minced

1 large green bell pepper, stemmed, seeded, and chopped small

3 ribs celery, washed well, white parts removed, and chopped small

4 cups of buttermilk cornbread (recipe page 42)

5 slices of white or wheat bread or crouton cubes for stuffing

1 can cream of chicken soup

1 cup chicken gizzards

3 large eggs

¼ cup of half and half

2 teaspoons celery salt

2 teaspoons seasoning salt

1 tablespoon dried sage

1 tablespoon poultry seasoning

2 cups chicken or turkey stock, or more as needed, (see recipe page 13)

1 cup shucked oysters, with their liquid

salt and freshly ground pepper to taste

Preheat the oven to 350° F.

Cook the gizzards in chicken stock until tender. Allow to cool. Drain and reserve the gizzards and chicken stock separately.

Heat the butter in a large fry pan and add the onions, bell peppers, and celery. Fry until onions and celery are softened. Remove from heat. Place in a large bowl.

Add the cornbread, plain bread or croutons, cream of chicken soup, gizzards, egg, and half and half. Mix well.

Add the celery salt, seasoning salt, sage, and poultry seasoning, and mix well. Add the chicken or turkey stock as needed for the dressing to be well moistened.

Add the oysters. Mix well and pour the mixture in to a buttered 9x13 baking dish. Bake for about 30–45 minutes until dressing is firm.

Sherrie Burrell suggests mixing the dressing the night before and refrigerating before baking—that the way the flavors have a chance to meld. Allow all of the ingredients to cool before mixing the dressing.

··· Who Are the Gullah/Geechee? ···

In 2004, the National Trust of Historic Preservation named the Gullah/Geechee coast as one of the 11 Most Endangered Historic Sites in America, fearing that encroachment on these communities will result in the extinction of the culture, its language, and customs.

Queen Quet, Chieftess of the Gullah/Geechee Nation and Dayclean, the African Spirit, lead an ancestral tribute ceremony at the Gullah/Geechee Reunion on Sullivan's Island, South

Follow the eastern coast of the United States to the South, where the water washes around the crags of the sea islands from Jacksonville, North Carolina to Jacksonville, Florida, and you will find the group of black Americans who are more directly connected to Mother Africa than perhaps any in the nation who descended from chattel slavery. They are the Gullah/Geechee people, whose ancestors were brought in chains to work the swampy and fetid rice, Sea Island cotton, and indigo plantations of the southeastern coastal region.

In addition to enduring the inhumanness of slavery, they also had to combat diseases like malaria and yellow fever, which were rampant in the rice fields they were forced to tend. Many of the enslaved Africans born on Africa's Rice Coast, which stretches primarily from what is now Senegal to Sierra Leone and Liberia on the continent's west coast, were immune to these illnesses. However, the white plantation owners were not, and they fled their profitable plantation lands, choosing instead to live on the mainland. The result was that many sea-island plantations were self-contained communities where the African people were autonomous, even as their knowledge was exploited to bring forth many of the cash crops and to build the buildings within the area.

On these plantations, with minimal interaction with their European masters, these enslaved Africans strengthened themselves and their African-combined African traditions. They mixed the ways of various ethic groups from their homelands and created a uniquely pan–African American culture with its own language, Gullah/Geechee, which is a type of Creole that is somewhat similar to the patois spoken in Jamaica, Barbados, Suriname, and Sierra Leone.

Due to a lack of true knowledge of these communities, for many years "Gullah" or "Geechee" were terms used separately by outsiders to describe what they considered to be different groups living in the region. However, Gullah/Geechees came together on July 2, 2000 to stand for their human right to self-determination, and began a movement of reconnection and recognition as one unique minority group. The Gullah/Geechee still practice African traditions for major life events, such as weddings, funerals, and births. They continue to make clay pots and sewn baskets in the African traditions, and their diet is still heavily based on rice and the seafood harvested from local waters. Purely African musical instruments, like the shegureh and various skin drums are still in use. Many celebrations are held throughout the year in the Gullah/Geechee Nation to celebrate their culture.

For more information on the Gullah/Geechee, visit **www.officialgullahgeechee.info.**

* *

"My fader gone to unknown land.
O de Lord he plant his garden deh.
He raise de fruit for you to eat.
He dat eat shall neber die."

— **From the oldest published version of the Gullah/Geechee spiritual,**
Michael Row Your Boat Ashore, **1867**

* *

Did You Know? *The popular children's stories about Brer Rabbit are actually African folktales retold among the Gullah/Geechee people?*

* *

Executive Office Catfish Curry

Washington, DC

SERVES 4

Food historian Adrian Miller believes Caribbean influence on American cuisine is often overlooked. In Martha Washington's Rules for Cookery, *one finds a fish curry recipe that is attributed to Elizabeth Monroe, the wife of President James Monroe, that most likely came to the colonies by way of the West Indies. Today, curry mixes unique to Jamaica, Trinidad, Barbados, and other islands comprise the base spice for many staple dishes. Mr. Miller learned the following updated recipe that celebrates the marriage of ingredients from the West Indies and the American South from a chef who created the dish to complement a presentation. "He pepped it up with ginger, garlic, bell peppers, carrots and celery, some heat (piquin chili), and a pinch of brown sugar."*

3 or 4 catfish fillets
1 quart water
2 onions
chopped parsley
1 tablespoon butter
1 tablespoon flour
2 teaspoons curry powder
salt and pepper to taste

Clean the catfish fillets and cut into to small pieces.

Over moderate heat, stew the water, fish, onions, parsley, salt, and pepper until the liquid is reduced to about 1 cup.

Remove the fish, cover to keep warm, and reserve.

Rub the butter with the flour, combine with the curry powder, and thicken the gravy with it.

Cook for a few minutes, stirring continuously.

Season with salt and pepper, pour over the fish, and serve immediately.[19]

Chef Jeff's Pan-Roasted Catfish

Las Vegas, Nevada

SERVES 4

"Catfish was a regular staple at granddaddy's Friday fish fry," says Chef Jeff Henderson. Grandad deep-fried the fish in a cornmeal breading, along with jumbo shrimp, red snapper and buffalo fish. He liked to change the sides regularly. Chef Jeff's favorite was the homemade fries and potato salad. His version of this family-style catfish offers a healthier option.

CATFISH

6–8 ounces farm-raised or wild catfish filets
1½ tablespoons vegetable oil
kosher salt to taste
cracked black pepper to taste

2 tablespoons of fresh thyme, finely chopped
kosher salt to taste
cracked black pepper to taste

Preheat oven to 350° F.

Rinse catfish fillets under cold running water, pat fish dry, and season with salt and pepper.

In a non-stick pan over medium heat, add vegetable oil. Once oil is hot, place catfish into pan. Cook until one side is golden brown, 2–3 minutes, then turn fish over. Remove pan from stove and place it in oven. Roast 10–12 minutes. Remove from oven and set aside.

Serve over Sautéed Succotash (page 149)

Sheila Chadwick's Stuffed Fish

Indianapolis, Indiana

SERVES 4

Source: Sheila Chadwick

Sheila Chadwick is a single parent who has often had to find economical and unique ways to prepare food for her daughters, Anetra and Ashlee. Her stuffed fish recipe was born out of her love for both fish and crab, but when she first made it she never thought the girls would eat it, so she only made enough for one. To her surprise, she says she can "clearly remember sitting the finished product on the counter and watching their mouths drool over it. Luckily for them I was willing to share!" This dish is now a huge hit in Ms. Chadwick's family. "This is the perfect dish for seafood lovers," she says. "It's easy to make and relatively inexpensive, yet the presentation looks as if you've spent all day preparing it."

2 1-pound pieces boneless fish, such as tilapia, snapper, catfish, or sole
8 ounces canned lump crabmeat
1 tablespoon mayonnaise
1 tablespoon melted butter
⅛ teaspoon sea salt
⅛ teaspoon black pepper
⅛ teaspoon Creole seasoning (page 235)
⅛ teaspoon garlic powder
1 8-ounce can cream of mushroom soup

Pass
It Down
TIP

To kick up this presentation a notch with a boost of extra flavor, sprinkle with some paprika or finely shopped parsley.

Preheat oven to 350° F. In a large bowl, combine the crab meat, mayonnaise, and butter and mix very well.

Add the sea salt, pepper, Creole seasoning, and garlic powder and mix well.

Spoon the crab mixture onto the fish, distributing primarily in the middle. Roll the pieces of fish over the crabmeat mixture and secure the piece closed with a toothpick.

Place the fish in aluminum foil and wrap it loosely, leaving an opening for the steam to escape. Place the package in a baking dish.

Bake for 20 minutes or until the flesh is firm and white. While the fish is cooking, heat the cream of mushroom soup in a saucepan. Do not add milk or water to the soup even if the label on the can calls for it.

Once the stuffed fish has completely cooked, remove it from the oven and allow to cool for 10 minutes. Place the pieces on a plate and gently remove the toothpicks. Spoon the mushroom soup over the top.

Giselle Colón-Wright's Mofongo Stuffed with Seafood Stew

SERVES 4

"In Africa and the Caribbean, the tradition of using a starchy vegetable as a hearty filler together with a broth or stew is a common feature of daily cuisine," writes Giselle Colón-Wright of this favorite family dish. *"Generally, in Africa, cassava or other root vegetables are used, but in the Caribbean plantains are often preferred. Whereas in Africa the starchy roots are typically beaten into a floury paste with mortar and pestle, served with a stew of meat and vegetables, in the Caribbean the plantains are fried and then mashed before serving. My father passed down this recipe to me, as it was one of his favorite dishes. Today, my husband helps to maintain it as a part of the food tradition in our family."*

MOFONGO
salt pork with skin (optional)
8 green plantains cut into 2-inch chunks
1 teaspoon salt
1 teaspoon adobo seasoning
4 large garlic cloves, crushed to a paste
1–1½ tablespoons olive oil
1 cup canola oil

SEAFOOD STUFFING
2 tablespoons olive oil
2 garlic cloves, crushed
1 medium yellow onion
2 cubanelle peppers
1 large ripe tomato
1 cup tomato sauce
½ cup white wine
1 pound of either shrimp, scallops or lump crab meat
1 tablespoon dried oregano
2 tablespoons capers
juice of ½ lemon or lime
2 tablespoons grated Parmesan cheese for garnish
1 bunch fresh cilantro, washed, stemmed, and chopped for garnish

MOFONGO

Heat a small fry pan and add the salt pork (if using). Fry until the fat is rendered and skin is crispy. Remove the salt pork from the pan with a slotted spoon and set aside on paper towels to drain.

Place the plantain pieces in a large saucepan with salt and adobo seasoning and bring to a boil. Simmer for 15 minutes, turn off the heat and cover for 15 minutes more.

Drain the green plantains from the pot and pat dry. Heat a large fry pan with the canola oil on medium-high heat and add the plantain pieces. Fry until lightly browned, about 1 minute per side. Remove from oil with a slotted spoon and reserve the oil.

Place the mofongo in a large mortar and pestle or food processor fitted with a plastic blade. Add the garlic paste and the cooked salt pork, along with 2 teaspoons of olive oil. Pound into a smooth paste or, if using a food processor, pulse into a thick, firm dough.

Form the mixture into balls the size of tennis balls and set aside until all are completed.

Reheat the canola oil in which you fried the green plantains. Add the mofongo balls and fry until the outside is crispy. Remove the mofongo balls from the heat and place on a platter. Make a deep indentation in the mofongo using the end of a wooden spoon or a pestle.

SEAFOOD STEW

Heat the olive oil in a large fry pan on medium-high heat and add the garlic, onion, peppers, and tomato. Cook until the onions become softened.

Lower the heat and add the wine and tomato sauce. Simmer until the liquid is reduced by one half.

Add the seafood, oregano, and capers, and mix well. Simmer for about 5–7 minutes or until the seafood is cooked through.

Add the lemon juice and Parmesan cheese. Remove from heat.

Fill the center of each mofongo with the seafood sauce and garnish with cilantro and grated Parmesan cheese. Serve hot.

Karilyn Parks' World's Best Salmon Patties

Decatur, Georgia

SERVES 4

Karilyn Parks grew up in the South hating most Southern dishes because, she says, her mom, who was not much of a cook, did not do them justice. "It wasn't until I started cooking that I realized it wasn't the food, but her lack of culinary skill," she says. Her recipe for salmon patties came out of a desire to turn the not-so-great version of the dish she remembers from childhood into something terrific and a little more healthful than her mother's deep-fried version.

1 15-ounce can of pink salmon
⅓ cup chopped celery
⅓ cup chopped scallions
2 eggs
1 tablespoon reduced-sodium soy sauce
1 cup Italian breadcrumbs
¾ cup plain breadcrumbs
1 teaspoon cayenne pepper
½ cup corn or canola oil

In a medium-size bowl, remove the skin and bones from the salmon and set aside.

Using a small fry pan, sauté the celery and scallions in one teaspoon of the oil until soft. Remove from heat and set aside.

In a small bowl, combine the two eggs and the soy sauce. Pour the egg mixture into the medium-size bowl with the salmon. Stir until well blended.

Stir in the remaining ingredients, starting with the Italian and plain breadcrumbs, then the scallions and celery, and finishing with the cayenne pepper.

Form the salmon mixture into medium-size round patties about 3 inches wide. Using a large fry pan, heat the remaining cooking oil. When the oil reaches 350° F or a bit of breadcrumbs dropped into oil bubbles vigorously, fry the patties at a low to medium-low heat for 5 minutes on each side or until golden brown.

Drain on a wire rack set over a cookie sheet or on a paper towel-lined plate and serve.

Zina Purnell's Spicy Seafood Pasta

Lithonia, Georgia

SERVES 4

"As a single working parent I had to come up with different ways to prepare food using whatever I had available in the kitchen with minimal cooking and prep time," says Zina Purnell. "I have always loved cooking, but everyday meals can become rather boring, and my daughter was not a lover of leftovers. One day I just decided to try something different using only what I had available in my kitchen. I just started mixing ingredients together based on smell and taste, and ended up with this dish. Seafood and pasta are two of my weaknesses and putting them together just sounded right."

2 tablespoons virgin olive oil
1½ each green, red, yellow bell peppers, stemmed, seeded, and sliced thinly
1 serrano chili pepper, stemmed, seeded, and sliced
2 cloves of garlic, sliced thinly
1¼ white onion, sliced thinly
1 package beef hot links, cut into bite-size pieces
1 large bottle Worcestershire sauce
1½ cups water
1½ pounds medium tiger shrimp, peeled and deveined
½ box spaghetti

Heat olive oil in a large fry pan on medium heat and add the bell peppers, Serrano chili pepper, onions, and garlic. Sauté, stirring often, until the peppers are soft, about 2–3 minutes.

Stir in the bottle of Worcestershire sauce and water. Bring mixture to a boil.

Heat another fry pan over medium heat and add the beef hot links. Cook until brown, stirring often, about 5 minutes. Remove pieces with a slotted spoon and add them to the Worcestershire sauce mixture.

Add the shrimp and turn heat down to low-medium. Cover and simmer 15–20 minutes.

Cook spaghetti per box directions and drain.

Place the spaghetti in a large bowl and pour the shrimp sauce mixture on top of it.

Zenzele Tanya Bell's Fried Fish

Albany, New York

SERVES 4

Tanya Bell, an IT consultant who lives in Albany, New York and is an avid knitter, skier, and photographer, grew up in Brooklyn, New York, where she says this fried fish was a staple of family gatherings. "My family has been frying fish this way since before I was born. My mom's side of the family is from an area called Swan Quarter in Hyde County, North Carolina, considered the 'inner banks,' meaning somewhere near the Outer Banks, and very close to water. My dad's side is from Atlantic City."

"Someone would always bring fish," Ms. Bell says. "The adults would stand over the sink, gutting fish on newspapers, while the kids would ooh and aah, or say something like 'That's nasty!' in the background. I thought for certain that I would learn the skill when I grew up, but the prevalence of the fillet made scaling fish obsolete."

1 pound white flaky fish fillet, such as tilapia or whiting
1 cup yellow cornmeal
½ teaspoon Old Bay Seasoning
¼ teaspoon black pepper
2 teaspoons garlic powder
1 cup canola oil for frying
salt to taste

Heat the oil in a large, deep fry pan over medium heat.

While oil is heating, mix the cornmeal, Old Bay Seasoning, black pepper, and garlic powder in a wide, shallow dish.

Coat the fillets in the cornmeal mixture and fry on medium-high heat until lightly brown on both sides, turning only once, 3–5 minutes per side.

Serve hot with salad or your favorite sides.

"Clean living keeps me in shape. Righteous thoughts are my secret—and New Orleans home cooking."

— Fats Domino

CHAPTER

5

Vegetables

Collard Greens with Smoked Pecans and Leeks

Harlem, New York

SERVES 4

Because Imani Wilson uses Koinonia hickory-smoked pecans, which are salted and spiced, these greens require minimal seasoning. If you're using other nuts, add salt and pepper to taste. This recipe works best with a 4-inch-deep sauté pan with a diameter of 10-inch or more.

6 bunches young collard greens
3 small leeks or 2 large leeks, to yield 1½ cups sliced
3 tablespoons olive oil
⅔ cup smoked pecans
3 cloves garlic, smashed
1 teaspoon red pepper flakes
3 cloves garlic, sliced
sea salt (optional)
freshly ground black pepper (optional)

Wash each collard leaf carefully both front and back and trim the stems off at the base of the leaves. Set aside.

Wash leeks and slice as thinly as possible. Stack ten collard leaves at a time, roll them tightly like a cigar. Using a chef's knife, slice fine ribbons from each cigar.

Heat pan over medium flame for a minute. Add the oil and pecans to the pan. Remove pecans with a slotted spoon when they've just begun to toast. Set pecans aside and add smashed garlic and leeks to pan.

When the aromatics have softened slightly, stir in the red pepper flakes. Stir well to incorporate. Add all the greens and cover for 10 minutes.

Remove cover, add garlic slices, and return the toasted pecans to the pan. Stir well. Cover and cook another 5 minutes. The greens should be bright green in color and retain a crisp texture. Season with sea salt and black pepper, to taste, and serve immediately. Yields 10–12 cups.

Ron Johnson's Crunchy Collards

Virginia Beach, Virginia

SERVES 4

Ron Johnson, an IT systems analyst for a major healthcare firm in southeastern Virginia, struggled with his weight and high blood pressure. He realized the only way to health was to change the way he ate. "My wife and I revisited all of our recipes and simply said, 'Don't change them. Let's just make them healthier!'" he says. A passionate home cook who dreams one day of opening a restaurant he plans to name after his late father, Mr. Johnson says he learned his cooking skills from always being in the kitchen as his parents cooked for him and his three younger sisters. His adaptations of family recipes include these crunchy collards, which he says are not your traditional collard greens. His new way of cooking has certainly paid off. "Since we started using healthier ingredients with our cooking along with other personal changes, I've lost 41 pounds and have never felt better!" he says.

1⅓ pounds collard greens, cleaned well, with thick stems removed
3 tablespoons extra virgin olive oil
1 cup minced, smoked turkey leg meat
¼ cup chopped garlic
3½ cups low-fat/low-sodium chicken broth
½ cup water
¼ cup vinegar
1 teaspoon sea salt
1 tablespoon black pepper
¼ cup maple syrup
1 tablespoon cayenne pepper (optional)

Place several collard greens on top of each other in a stack and roll them up like a cigar. Slice the roll in 1-inch sections. Repeat with all the greens. Place the cigars in a big bowl, cover with paper towels, and set in the fridge until ready.

Place the turkey meat in a large bowl and add the garlic. Mix well.

Heat a medium-size fry pan on medium-high and add the olive oil. Add turkey and garlic mixture and fry over medium heat 6–8 minutes or until the turkey pieces start to brown.

In a large saucepan, add chicken broth, water, and vinegar, and heat on medium-high heat. When the mixture just comes to a boil, add the turkey mixture. In a stockpot, add chicken broth, water, and vinegar. Stir in the salt and pepper. Allow the mixture to simmer 2–4 minutes and add collard greens. Stir well, cover, and cook 30 minutes.

Add maple syrup and cayenne pepper, if using, turn heat down to medium, and toss the greens around again. Cover and cook about 1 more hour (tossing occasionally).

··· The Kitchen Garden ···

PLOTTING THE PAST AND FUTURE

BY MICHAEL TWITTY

Source: Library of Congress

Michael Twitty is an African American foodways historian who worked with D. Landreth Seed Company to develop the African American heritage collection. Read more about him in the essay "Finding My Way Home," on page 15.

From earliest colonial times, African Americans tended the plantation kitchen gardens and small gardens in their homesteads, and then took those goods to market.

In West and Central Africa, members of every caste and class had small, productive gardens within the home compound. These were used largely to produce fruits, vegetables, and condiments that enhanced a diet based on pounded starches and soups and stews. Even members of traditional societies that were enslaved regarded their kitchen gardens and subsistence plots as a right rather than a privilege.

Despite being brought to the Americas as slaves, Africans kept their tradition that said that everybody, including those enslaved or indentured, had a right to the cultivation of the land for the sake of their household. This tradition helped shape the contours of the African American experience in slavery. From Caribbean plots on mountainsides to acres of land in the woods to plots near cabins—gardens thrived in the enslaved communities.

Having a garden was a major element of cultural and social empowerment. These plots allowed enslaved people to control part of their food supply, grow healthy food, and give them some sense of ownership. Gardens provided many with the means to barter their goods and produce and sell them for money. At Monticello there are extensive records showing that Thomas Jefferson's workforce sold him a wide variety of produce from their own personal plots.

Access to markets in towns and cities enabled enslaved blacks to communicate with the outside world, providing contacts and the potential for freedom. Every member of the family put time into these plots—some by daylight, some by moonlight and torch.

Many of these gardens were based on companion planting—growing plants that complement each other's growth. And intercropping—planting more than one crop in the same mound or row rather than in individual sections—was the rule. This reduced insects, preserved water, conserved space, and helped retain and enhance soil nutrients. Our ancestors were colonial America's premier organic farmers. Any ashes, bones, and other "waste" would have been used to keep the garden fertile.

There is no "typical" produce list for enslaved people's gardens. These plots certainly helped preserve African food traditions even as new foods from the Americas and Europe were incorporated into the diet of the enslaved community. Many of these foods had already made inroads in West and Central Africa, and were already familiar to enslaved Africans and their descendants. By the 18th century, corn, pumpkins, squashes, gourds, sweet potatoes, white potatoes, peanuts, black-eyed peas, beans, watermelons, muskmelons, and sorghum seeds would be left for future generations to find in archaeological digs.

From the same period onward, enslaved African Americans are described growing peppers, okra, onions, cabbage, collards, turnips and turnip greens, rice, sesame, tomatoes, herbs, and other crops. These garden plots would prevail throughout Southern rural history. As African Americans migrated to Southern cities and moved north and west, however, it became harder to maintain the garden-ways of the South, but in many urban community gardens this ancient tradition is preserved today.

For tips on pickling, canning, and preserving the bounty of your own garden, see Tips for Boiling Water Bath Canning (page 228).

"I was born in Newberry County, near Chappelle Depot. My master in slavery time was John Boazman . . . The folks back home had fine farms, good gardens, and took pride in raising all kinds of things in the garden. They allus planted Irish potatoes the second time in one season."

**— Ex-slave Caroline Farrow,
Newberry, South Carolina, 1937**

Courtesy: *Born in Slavery: Slave Narratives from the Federal Writers' Project, 1936-1938*,
Library of Congress American Memory Collection

··· Community Gardens ···

BY CHAZ FOSTER-KYSER

Source: West End Community Gardens

Chaz Foster-Kyser is a New York–based writer, editor, and vegetarian who loves shopping at local farmer's markets and is a big supporter of urban farming. She is the author of Embracing the Real World: The Black Woman's Guide to Life After College.

West End Community Gardens, affectionately known as "we garden," is an example of African Americans' ongoing commitment to feed those within the community using their own land, labor, and knowledge of crop cultivation. Located in Birmingham, Alabama, the garden was created in 2008 through the joint effort of Urban Ministry, a non-profit that provides philanthropic services to West End residents, and Community Church Without Walls, a church that meets in the homes of its members.

Like many urban areas, West End is largely devoid of the type of services and businesses that make a community viable, such as grocery stores with fresh and inexpensive food. Childhood obesity, high blood pressure, and diabetes due in part to this inequality are among the many health issues people within West End contend with. Yet West End Gardens is not only helping to alleviate these issues, it is bringing community members together in the process. The "green" gathering rests on a half-acre city lot and has three common garden areas used to raise vegetables that can be sold at markets and to local restaurants. It also houses 16 community plots that residents can utilize through volunteering or by leasing for a nominal fee. Gardeners are furnished with soil, natural fertilizers, seed, seedlings, and basic organic gardening instruction. There are even six "baby boxes" for young children to use as they learn how to grow their own plants.

The West End Gardens boasts foods ranging from arugula to yams and a variety of field peas, peppers, and tomatoes. It is especially known for its 12-foot-tall okra as well as its collard greens, highlighted during the garden's annual Collard Green Cook-Off.

The prized garden is as beautiful as it is bountiful, as herbs and flowers grow alongside fruits and vegetables. And just like community gardeners of yesterday, members consistently practice companion planting and crop rotation. They also make their own compost, which is generously incorporated into the garden beds.

The garden has been so successful that members have formed a Community Gardening Resource Team to assist others with starting gardens—demonstrating the "each-one-teach-one" belief needed to keep community gardens a part of African Americans' history and future.

Community gardens enrich the lives of people living in other urban areas across the United States as well, often receiving support from city governments, universities, and non-profit organizations. In Detroit, many trash-strewn vacant lots have been transformed into community gardens through the Garden Resource Program, an initiative sponsored by The Greening of Detroit, the Detroit Agriculture Network, EarthWorks Urban Farm/Capuchin Soup Kitchen, and Michigan State University. Together, they provide residents with the supplies and resources needed to grow fruits and vegetables. When the program was first implemented in 2004, Detroit had 80 registered urban gardens. Today, more than 700 are spread throughout the city.

To learn more about community gardens, visit the American Community Gardening Association's website, **www.communitygarden.org.**

• •

"I have found that the way to a community's heart is truly through its stomach. Feed a community well and they respond in kind. The simple act of planting a garden has transformed my life."

— **Ama Shambulia,**
West End Community Gardens' Program Director

• •

Monticello Okra & Tomatoes

Charlottesville, Virginia

SERVES 6 TO 8

Thomas Jefferson was very familiar with okra—a plant native to West Africa that was transported to the Americas during the transatlantic slave trade—and grew it in his garden at Monticello. Here's a classic combination of Southern vegetables that is especially popular during the summer months, and could have likely been prepared for the third president by his slave-cook Peter Hemings.

4 tablespoons olive oil (or bacon grease)
2 pounds okra, sliced (fresh or frozen)
2 cups tomatoes, peeled (fresh or canned)
1 large onion, chopped
1 tablespoon fresh lemon juice
1 tablespoon Worcestershire sauce
1 tablespoon sugar
1 teaspoon salt
⅛ teaspoon dried oregano
⅛ teaspoon dried basil
1 teaspoon black or cayenne pepper

If using frozen okra, first bring to room temperature.

Heat olive oil in a large, heavy skillet over medium heat.

Slightly lower the heat, add okra, and sauté gently for a few minutes.

Stir okra frequently to keep it from sticking.

Add tomatoes, onion, lemon juice, Worcestershire sauce, sugar, salt, oregano, basil, and black or cayenne pepper.

Toss all these together until there is virtually no liquid left in the pan.

Serve.

Haitian Hash

SERVES 6 TO 8

This is Ron Duprat's family recipe for hash, learned in his family kitchen in Haiti. Duprat, the author of My Journey of Cooking, says it is a lovely side dish for eggs and omelettes, or grilled chicken, fish, or steak.

Most of the nutrients in potatoes are in the skin, including iron and other important minerals. As long as the potatoes are well scrubbed before boiling, try making this recipe with the skin on.

1 pound Yukon Gold potatoes
1 pound sweet potatoes
1 pound boniato potatoes
½ cup extra virgin olive oil
1 Vidalia onion, stemmed, seeded, and chopped
1 red bell pepper, stemmed, seeded, and chopped
1 yellow bell pepper, stemmed, seeded, and chopped
1 green bell pepper, stemmed, seeded, and chopped
2 Scotch bonnet (habañero) peppers, stemmed seeded, and minced
1 teaspoon Maldon or other sea salt
1 teaspoon freshly ground black pepper

Wash the potatoes well and place them in a large pot with enough water to cover by 3 inches. Bring water to a boil and lower to simmer for 25 minutes or until they're fork tender. Drain the potatoes and run cool water over them. When they're cool enough to handle, peel and chop into ½-inch pieces.

Heat olive oil in a medium sauté pan and add potatoes, onion, and all the bell peppers. Fry until onion is translucent. Add the Scotch bonnet peppers and stir well.

Season with salt and pepper. Serve as a side dish.

Did you know? *Boniato potatoes are also commonly called Cuban sweet potatoes, white sweet potatoes, or batata. They're most commonly eaten in tropical areas, like the Caribbean and Central and South America.*

Gillian Clark's Easy Corn Relish

Washington, DC

SERVES 4 TO 6

In a past life, Gillian Clark was a marketing executive, a stressful job that, she says, had her "drinking Mylanta" out of a bottle nightly. She cooked to relax, and in 1995 with a one-year-old and six-year-old, she decided to leave the marketing biz and go to cooking school. Entering the market at a time when chefs were not revered as they are today, she had to work two jobs to survive. Today, Chef Clark is executive chef and owner of The General Store and Post Office Tavern and the soon-to-open Georgia Avenue Meeting House. She makes this corn relish most often with crab cakes, but it is a fresh side dish for any summer menu.

6 ears of corn, shucked, cleaned, and carefully cut off of the cob
1 cup cider vinegar
3 tablespoons whole cloves
1 stick cinnamon
⅓ cup light brown sugar
salt and pepper
1 large red onion, finely diced
1 jalapeño pepper, finely diced
2 tablespoons finely chopped parsley

In a saucepan, bring vinegar, sugar, cloves, and cinnamon to a boil. Set aside and let cool slightly.

Place the corn kernels in a 2-quart pot and cover with cold water. Bring to a boil and then remove from heat and drain.

Put corn in a large bowl and add red onion, jalapeño pepper, and parsley to corn and mix well. Strain vinegar mixture and pour over corn mixture. Mix well.

Season with salt and pepper. Set aside in fridge to completely chill.

Did you know? *George Crum, an African American-Native American cook at Moon's Lake House, is credited with inventing the potato chip? In 1853, the then-posh resort in fashionable Saratoga Springs in upstate New York catered to a wealthy clientele, one of whom complained that Crum's French Fried potatoes were too thick. To teach the customer a lesson, Crum sliced the potatoes as thinly as possible, deep fried them in oil, and doused them with salt—much to the customer's delight. The crisps became so popular they were branded Saratoga Chips and widely sold as a snack. Earlier English recipe books had recipes for "potato shavings," so while it's just possible that the cook didn't actually invent the treat, there is no doubt that he—and his legendary showmanship—popularized it into what is now one of America's most beloved snacks.*

Edna Lewis' Corn Pudding

Freetown, Virginia

SERVES 6 TO 8

Edna Lewis can easily be called the Julia Child of Southern cuisine—and in fact she often has. The granddaughter of a former slave, Ms. Lewis was born and raised in Virginia, but moved to New York City at the age of 16. She lived a remarkable life, first as a seamstress working for notable celebrities, then as a political activist and later as a noted chef.

This recipe for a classic corn pudding is from her first cookbook, The Taste of Country Cooking, *in which she writes, "Corn pudding was one of the great delicacies of summer and the first corn dish of the season. After helping to thin out corn and weed it, we watched eagerly for the day when Mother served her rich, aromatic, golden-brown corn pudding. It was always served with a sweet potato casserole made from fresh-dug sweet potatoes." The recipe is reprinted as the author wrote it.*

2 cups corn, cut from the cob
⅓ cup sugar
1 teaspoon salt
2 eggs, beaten
2 cups rich (whole) milk
3 tablespoons melted butter
½ teaspoon fresh-grated nutmeg
1½ quart casserole

Author's note: An ingenious way we had to retain the freshness of the corn was to stand the ears in a tub of water about 2½ inches deep. When the ear is severed from the stalk, its source of moisture is cut off. By standing the corn in a dish of clean water, the cob continues to absorb moisture. Refrigeration, of course, helps. How many ears will your icebox hold?

Cut corn from the cob into a mixing bowl by slicing from the top of the ear downward. Don't go too close to the cob—cut only half of the kernel. Scrape the rest off. This gives a better texture the pudding.

Sprinkle in the sugar and salt, stir well. Mix the beaten eggs and milk together, and pour the mixture into the corn. Add the melted butter. Mix thoroughly and spoon the mixture in to a well-buttered casserole.

Sprinkle over with nutmeg. Set the casserole into a pan of hot water and set this into a preheated 350° F oven for 35 to 40 minutes or until set. Test by inserting a clean knife into the center of the pudding. If it comes out clean it's done.

Dr. George Washington Carver

Dr. George Washington Carver, M.S. AGR., D.Sc., Director, Experiment Station, Tuskegee Institute, is most known for his work with peanuts, but his work as a horticulturist extended to making the most of poor soil for sustenance crops that could be put to both edible and non-edible use. These included not just the peanut, but soybeans, cowpeas, and sweet potatoes. Dr. Carver's sweet potato wisdom, originally shared in the 1920s is still informative and inspiring today.

"There are but few if any of our staple farm crops receiving more attention than the sweet potato, and indeed rightfully so—the splendid service it rendered during the great World War in the saving of wheat flour, will not soon be forgotten. The 118 different and attractive products (to date) made from it, are sufficient to convince the most skeptical that we are just beginning to discover the real value and marvelous possibilities of this splendid vegetable.

Here in the South, there are but few if any farm crops that can be depended upon one year with another for satisfactory yields, as is true of the sweet potato. It is also true that most of our southern soils produce potatoes superior in quality, attractive in appearance and satisfactory in yields, as any other section of the country."

"As a food for human consumption, the sweet potato has been, and always will be, held in very high esteem and its popularity will increase in this direction as we learn more about its many possibilities.

There is an idea prevalent that anybody can cook sweet potatoes. This is a very great mistake, and the many, many dishes of ill-cooked potatoes that are placed before me as I travel over the South prompt me to believe that these recipes will be of value (many of which I have copied verbatim from Bulletin No. 129, U. S. Department of Agriculture). The above bulletin so aptly adds the following:

The delicate flavor of a sweet potato is lost if it is not cooked properly. Steaming develops and preserves the flavor better than boiling, and baking better than steaming. A sweet potato cooked quickly is not well cooked. Time is an essential element. Twenty minutes may serve to bake a sweet potato so that a hungry man can eat it, but if the flavor is an object, it should be kept in the oven for an hour."

Dr. Carver's Sweet Potato Croquettes

Tuskegee, Alabama

SERVES 4

2 cups mashed, boiled, steamed, or baked sweet potatoes
2 egg yolks
1 whole egg
1½–2 cups fresh breadcrumbs
lard or oil
salt to taste

Put sweet potatoes and beaten yolks of two eggs in a pot, and season to taste.

Stir over medium fire until the mixture pulls away from the sides of the pot.

Let sit covered in refrigerator for 1 hour.

When cold form into small croquettes. Roll potato balls in egg and breadcrumbs, and fry in hot oil to amber color.

Serve.

Sweet Potatoes Baked With Apples

Tuskegee, Alabama

SERVES 4

4 medium-size sweet potatoes
4 medium-size apples
1½ cups sugar
1½ cups butter cut into slices
¾ pint hot water
salt to taste

Wash, peel, and cut the potatoes in slices about ¼ of an inch thick.

Pare and slice the apples in the same way.

Put potatoes and apples in baking dish in alternate layers.

Sprinkle sugar and butter over the top, along with hot water.

Bake slowly at 350° F for one hour.

Serve steaming hot.

··· A Taste for the Past ···

BY GUY-OREIDO WESTON

Guy-Oreido Weston is an HIV program consultant living in the Washington DC area. His passion for researching the remarkable history of his ancestors of Timbuctoo has culminated in a lifelong project and various writings.

Even as a child, my favorite people were the matriarchs in my life: my mother, mother's friends, grandmothers, grandmothers' sisters, and their female cousins. Among these women, the person who left me the most lasting legacy was Lillian Giles Gardner, my maternal grandmother's first cousin. Lillian was an elegant, beautiful, and youthful woman at every age. A retired jazz vocalist, she was progressive and open-minded in an era when the norm was respecting the status quo. While most of the Giles family was Methodist or Baptist, Lillian was Episcopalian. I think my siblings and I looked up to Lillian because she was "different." As teenagers, she made us feel comfortable discussing things we felt we couldn't discuss with our parents.

Among all of the cooking women in the Giles family, in my mind, Lillian was the most gifted. In addition to the "down home" recipes of corn pudding, candied sweet potatoes, fresh collard greens, succotash, stewed tomatoes from scratch, and a variety of cakes and deep dish pies, Lillian could make soufflés and various gourmet recipes. So if I needed pointers on cooking something, Lillian was right up there with my mother as a go-to. As a young adult living on my own for the first time, I began calling Lillian more often. One day, when I needed a recipe for a distinctive dessert, she gave me an applesauce cake recipe that still gets rave reviews whenever I make it. Eventually, she gave me a 1950s-era Betty Crocker cookbook that continues to be my primary cooking reference to this day.

But the most enduring legacy was not the cookbook. Lillian was also the guardian of the old, rural, family homestead. She was the first family member to tell me and my siblings about it when I was 13. No one had lived there since the 1930s, and the house was gone long before I was born. Fortunately, various relatives had kept up the taxes for more than 60 years, sometimes not laying eyes on it for a decade or more. I knew my great-grandmother was born there in 1902, but I had no idea that she was the fourth generation to live at the site.

The area where our homestead was is called Timbuctoo, located in Westampton Township in southern New Jersey. Although most county residents may have never heard of it, it appears on area maps under that name to this day. It was founded by freed blacks and runaway slaves around 1820 with the support of local Quakers.

At its peak in the mid-1800s, Timbuctoo had more than 125 residents, a school, an AME Zion Church, and a cemetery. It was also a stop on the Underground Railroad. Today, only the cemetery remains, which contains the graves of black Civil War veterans.

When I saw Timbuctoo for the first time as a teenager, it was anything but a historic site. The grass on our 1.25-acre lot was waist high. The adjacent lot had a dilapidated old house with an abandoned 1962 Ford Galaxy next to it. That was around 1975. Over the next few years, I would ride by that lot from time to time and just stare into the pasture and wonder what it must have been like to grow up there in the early 20th century.

One day in the mid-1980s, my mother and I went to visit Lillian. She had decided that she wanted to transfer the land to a younger generation, and she would begin by sharing various documents related to the property. She pulled out a rather non-descript manila envelope that contained the original 1829 deed from when my great, great, great, great grandfather bought his first parcel for $30. There was also a deed for an adjacent parcel purchased in 1831 for $8.50, a will from 1842, mortgage documents from 1845, and various receipts for mortgage payments and taxes through the 1930s.

The bits of papers intrigued me, luring me into the past, and I quickly became an amateur genealogist and learned all kinds of details about my ancestor's lives, including the birth of my great-great-great-great grandmother in Philadelphia around 1798, and her family's involvement in co-founding Mother Bethel AME Church in Philadelphia in 1794. I was absolutely fascinated. Eventually, I built a house in Timbuctoo and spent hours captivated by scenic, wooded vistas, roaming rabbits and chipmunks, and an occasional trespassing deer. My 74-year-old mother, Mary Giles Weston, and her various grandchildren—my nieces and nephew—volunteer at what is now an archeological site, unearthing Timbuctoo's past, managed under the auspices of Westampton Township and Temple University.

As for myself, I like to sit under a 130-year-old tree in our yard and contemplate what life must have been like during the latter years of the 19th century, when that very tree provided shade to my great-great grandfather and his children on hot summer days. For this experience, I will be forever indebted to my cousin Lillian, who gave me a cookbook, as well as a tangible parcel of history and an indelible impression of the meaning of family.

Lillian Jackson's Fried Green Tomatoes

Covert, Michigan

SERVES 4

Elizabeth "Charli" Bracken gave us this recipe from her grandmother Lillian Jackson, who once had a tomato garden and plenty of green tomatoes. "She would make fried green tomatoes you could smell miles away," says Ms. Bracken. "When I re-create her fried green tomatoes, my mind clearly takes me back to the wooden porch swing with a pitcher of cold, fresh-squeezed lemonade. I immediately appreciate the good old days when I enjoy this dish." Ms. Bracken's version has a dash of cayenne pepper for a little extra heat.

4 medium-size green tomatoes
1 teaspoon salt
4 egg whites
¼ cup milk
1 teaspoon onion powder
1 teaspoon garlic powder
1 teaspoon cayenne pepper
1 teaspoon paprika
½ cup yellow cornmeal
¼ cup flour
1 teaspoon white pepper
½ cup canola oil

Rinse and slice tomatoes in ¼-thick rounds and sprinkle with ½ teaspoon of the salt. Allow tomatoes to sit while you prepare the dry and wet mixture.

In a small dish, slightly beat egg whites and milk, add onion powder, garlic powder, cayenne pepper, paprika, and ½ of the teaspoon of salt. Set aside.

In another small bowl combine cornmeal, flour, and white pepper.

Heat the canola oil in a medium skillet on medium heat.

Dip tomatoes in egg mixture, then the flour mixture until completely coated.

Slowly place tomatoes in hot oil and turn each side until lightly brown, about 5 minutes on a side. Place on wire rack set over a cookie sheet or a paper towel-lined plate. Use the remaining salt to season to taste.

Geri Bell's Stewed Tomato Casserole

Albany, New York

SERVES 6 TO 8

"We use tomatoes that someone in our family preserved, and I usually make it with one large mason jar of tomatoes, juice included," says Geri Bell of her family's tomato casserole. *"I'm guessing two average-sized store-bought cans will work just as well."*

2 cans stewed tomatoes, 14 ounces each
2 slices day-old bread, cut into 1-inch pieces (use an artisanal-style bread)
1 tablespoon sugar
⅛ teaspoon cinnamon
½ teaspoon nutmeg
1 tablespoon butter, cut into small pieces

Preheat oven to 350° F and grease an 8x8 baking dish.

In a large bowl, combine the tomatoes, sugar, cinnamon, and nutmeg. Mix well.

Add the bread pieces to the tomatoes. Stir well and pour into the greased baking dish. Dot the top of the mixture with pieces of butter. Bake until browned, about 30 minutes.

Serve hot.

BRIDGING DIVIDES ACROSS THE TABLE

When the school segregation issue was taken up by the federal court in Charlotte, the school board was ordered to give people in the community a chance to have their say. I was involved with a group called the Quality Education Committee . . .

There were some very conservative antibusing people, liberal whites, outspoken blacks, and so forth—mortal enemies, you might say—and getting them to associate with one another at all was a big problem. Our idea was to invite representatives of all the groups to a covered dish dinner, thinking that, regardless of race or politics or whatever, Southerners have always been brought up to be nice at the table . . .

. . . I don't remember what we had to eat. I guess I was too nervous to think about that. Everyone was ill at ease at first, but soon after we sat down you could feel the conversation level rising in the room. It was a very pleasant sound, and it told us that our idea was working.

— Maggie Ray; Charlotte, North Carolina
1985 interview, excerpt from
Southern Food: At home, on the Road, in History
by John Egerton, Ann Bleidt Egerton
University of North Carolina Press, A Chapel Hill Book, June 1993

··· Taking Back the Table ···

BY RAMIN GANESHRAM

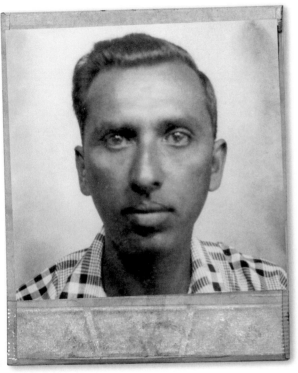

Ramin Ganeshram's father, Kris.

Ramin Ganeshram, the co-editor of the America I AM Pass It Down Cookbook *is a journalist, chef, and well-known authority on Caribbean cuisine. She writes about food from the perspective of cultural history, transition, and progression. Ms. Ganeshram is the author of* Sweet Hands: Island Cooking from Trinidad & Tobago *and* Stir It Up!*, a culinary novel for middle-grade readers published by Scholastic Press.*

When my father, Kris, came to the United States from his home country of Trinidad & Tobago in 1954, he took it into his head to see America. He envisioned driving through amber waves of grain, standing in awe of purple mountain majesties, and being welcomed on the front porches and at the kitchen tables of folks eager to tell their stories and eager to hear his own.

Although raised under English colonial rule, he was a brown man from a brown country whose day-to-day contacts with the nation's foreign masters were few and far between. He lived in a dark-hued world where separation by color was not exactly foreign, but was reserved for upper classes who might have more cause to butt up against the British ruling class.

Vegetables

As he took off with a white friend, a fellow schoolmate from Brooklyn College—crossing the Brooklyn Bridge into Manhattan and the George Washington Bridge into New Jersey and heading for points south—my father had no way of knowing that the most common citizen he would actually encounter was Jim Crow.

By the time he told me this story, some twenty years after it occurred, he only spoke with sadness, though at the time I know he raged against having to urinate on the sides of the road and sleep in the car while his friend found warm beds

On February 1, 1960, four African American college students sat down at a "whites only" Woolworth's lunch counter in Greensboro, North Carolina, and politely asked to be served. Though the items were available for sale—sodas, coffee, doughnuts—their request was denied and they were asked to leave. They remained in their seats, however. The next day, they returned and asked for service again, despite being sneered at, manhandled, and refused food. Their peaceful sit-down to challenge segregation helped ignite a movement to challenge racial inequality throughout the South.

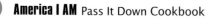

inside welcoming motels. Perhaps in moments of weariness he convinced himself that these indignities were not far different from visiting the bush communities on his native island, where there was no running water, and folks, though welcoming, rarely had an extra bed or cot on which a visitor could sleep.

He coped.

But what he could not cope with, what laid him low three times a day like clockwork, were the mealtimes. It was not simply that he couldn't find places that would serve him food—his friend could bring the meal out to the car—it was that he was denied the fellowship of the table. Unable to socialize and interact with his fellow man for stretches of miles and days at a time, he retreated into a sense of isolation he had never before experienced. Even back in Brooklyn, where my father had made his new home, the dining table was often a racially charged expanse. One day he and a family friend with whom he was staying went to a local luncheonette to eat. They were the only people of color there. On his way out, he saw the bus boy and waitress breaking the dishes they ate on rather than washing them so they could be reused.

In Trinidad, as in Africa, the Middle East, India, and the ancient world, it is an honor to share your table with a guest. Despite language barriers and differences of religion, tribal communities always held their tent flaps open for a stray visitor. An extra portion of food was always prepared, in case someone in need of fellowship and succor came to your door. In my father's childhood that golden rule was adhered to, even if it meant feeding the guest the only food you had.

When he returned to New York, after being abandoned on the roadside of Las Vegas when his companion could no longer take the stress of traveling with a colored man, my father became an active member of the NAACP and a civil rights marcher, eating along the route the foods cooked by intrepid church ladies, the cooks who nourished the movement. In fellowship he partook of their meals, a somber but hopeful stepchild of a church picnic or social.

It was, he said, the memory of those meals eaten alone, the dehumanization he felt being denied a place at the table, that spurred him on. Nothing delighted him more than the civil rights protests at lunch counters across the country. It was, to him, the most integral of victories—this taking back a place at the table. It represented not just the toppling of one of the bulwarks of segregation, but the ultimate measure of equality and possibility for understanding—for who can break bread and pass a piece to another person, fingers brushing in the transaction, and remain convinced that one is human and the other is not?

The Ganeshram's Trinidad Breadfruit Oil-Down

New York, New York

SERVES 4

In Pass It Down editor Ramin Ganeshram's father's country of Trinidad, breadfruit is a starchy tree fruit that was a mainstay for slaves and indentured laborers because it was filling but cheap for plantation owners to provide. It was often flavored with an equally cheap cut of pork, such as pig's feet.

    "Oil-down" refers to the African cooking method by which vegetables are stewed in coconut milk until all of the milk is absorbed and just a bit of coconut oil is left in the bottom of the pan. Smoked ham, bacon, or turkey bacon provides good flavor in this dish, but purely vegetarian versions are just as good. This recipe is reprinted, with permission, from Sweet Hands: Island Cooking from Trinidad & Tobago *(Hippocrene Books, 2010).*

1 tablespoon canola oil
1 large onion, minced
1 fresh pimiento pepper, stemmed, seeded, and chopped, or 1 teaspoon paprika
1 clove garlic, minced
¼ pound smoked bacon or turkey bacon, diced (optional)
3 scallions, finely chopped
½ Scotch bonnet or other hot red chili pepper, stemmed, seeded, and minced
1 teaspoon fresh thyme, or ½ teaspoon dried
4 cups coconut milk
1 large breadfruit, peeled, seeded, and chopped into large chunks**
coarse or kosher salt and freshly ground black pepper to taste

Heat the canola oil in a deep saucepan and add the onion and pimiento pepper. (If using paprika, add with the coconut milk.) Sauté until soft. Add the garlic and bacon and sauté for 1 minute more.

Add the scallions, hot pepper, and thyme, and sauté for 1 minute, stirring constantly. Stir in the coconut milk (and paprika if using) and bring to a boil.

Mix in the breadfruit and salt and black pepper to taste. Lower the heat and cover. Simmer for 30–40 minutes, or until the breadfruit has absorbed all the coconut milk. Serve hot.

** Breadfruit is available canned. One 16-ounce can is roughly equivalent to one fresh breadfruit. Drain well before using.

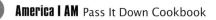

Chef Jeff's Sautéed Succotash

Las Vegas, Nevada

SERVES 4 TO 6

Chef Jeff Henderson says that as a child, he did not like a lot of vegetables, but his grandparents made sure he ate them often. "When I had a choice, it was all about the succotash: several Southern vegetables sautéed with some good ham pieces."

3 tablespoons unsalted butter
4 tablespoons fresh garlic, finely minced
2 medium shallots, finely diced
1½ cups diced ham
2 cups fresh corn, off the cob
1 cup okra
1 cup canned or fresh lima beans
1 cup fresh diced tomatoes
2 cups preboiled baby potatoes, cut into quarters
1 medium red bell pepper, diced small
3 tablespoons fresh, flat-leaf parsley, roughly chopped

In a skillet or non-stick sauté pan, melt butter over medium heat, then add garlic and shallots.

After about a minute, add diced ham, all the vegetables and the potatoes. Let cook 10–12 minutes or until vegetables are tender and caramelized, occasionally stirring.

Remove from heat. Stir in parsley and thyme and season with salt and pepper.

Serve immediately with Pan-Roasted Catfish (page 111).

Kevono's Spinach and Eggplant Lasagna

SERVES 10

Source: Kevono Hunt

Kevono Hunt has always enjoyed cooking for friends and family. This recipe was created shortly after his move to New York for one of his vegetarian friends. "She was begging me to cook something," Kevono says, "so I decided to make her some lasagna using two of her favorite foods— spinach and eggplant. Being the cook that I am, I created something simple and easy so she could replicate it."

4 cups water

2½ tablespoons of kosher salt

½ cup apple cider vinegar

2 bunches spinach

½ cup extra virgin olive oil

1 medium-sized eggplant, cut into ⅓-inch circular pieces

½ cup bell peppers in assorted colors, cut in small slivers

1 medium onion, cut in small slivers

¼ cup mushrooms

¼ teaspoon cinnamon

¼ teaspoon cardamom

¼ teaspoon paprika

½ tablespoon black pepper

½ cup white wine

1 package precooked lasagna pasta

1 12-ounce can of black beans

2 cups shredded mozzarella

2 pints ricotta cheese

2 jars of marinara sauce

4 garlic cloves

4 roma tomatoes, thinly sliced

1 sprig of rosemary

In a 4-quart pot, bring the 4 cups of water to a boil and add salt and apple cider vinegar. Clean and cut stems on spinach and place in water until the spinach changes to a rich green color, then place in an ice bath. Set aside for later.

Coat eggplant generously in olive oil and sprinkle with salt. Sear the eggplant until brown. Set aside.

Sauté the bell peppers and onions in olive oil, then add mushrooms and half of all seasonings. After 3 minutes, add white wine and let reduce. Set aside.

Cook the pasta according to the instructions on the box. Set aside.

In a lasagna pan, put ½ tablespoon of olive oil in the bottom and cover with black beans. Place eggplant on top of beans. Cover eggplant with ½ cup of mozzarella and spread ricotta over eggplant. Cover with marinara sauce. Place spinach on next layer and season with remaining seasonings. Coat with ricotta cheese and marinara sauce and another layer of pasta. Place sautéed bell peppers, onions, and mushroom on top and cover with ricotta and marinara sauce and the last of the pasta. Spread the remainder of the marinara sauce on top. Coat with ricotta and mozzarella.

Place roma tomatoes on top of mozzarella. Garnish with rosemary.

Bake lasagna in oven at 350° F for about 1 hour or until it reaches an internal temperature of 145° F.

Desmonette Hazly's Roasted Summer Vegetable Medley

Los Angeles, California

SERVES 4 TO 6

Dr. Desmonette Hazly is a social entrepreneur and community culinary arts instructor. She says she went to cooking school so she could help her community. "I have incorporated culinary arts as my primary tool for social change and community advocacy," says Dr. Hazly. "I use culinary arts to teach respect and self-worth to gang members, life skills and nutrition for teen moms, literacy and dignity to those who cannot read or write." Her summer vegetable medley is easy to prepare and a great way to introduce healthful eating to anyone, no matter what their level of skill in the kitchen. Read more about Dr. Hazly's work in the Summer Night Lights program in Sacred Table, Sacred Feast. (page 265)

3 zucchinis, sliced ¼-inch thick
2 yellow squash, sliced into ¼ thick pieces
3 red bell peppers, cut into ½-inch chunks
5 firm Roma tomatoes, cut into ½-inch chunks
2 cups fresh or frozen corn kernels
1½ cups Italian salad dressing
½ cup balsamic vinegar
salt and pepper to taste

Preheat oven to 400° F.

Place all vegetables in a baking pan and add Italian dressing and balsamic vinegar.

Toss vegetables until they're fully coated with the liquids. Season with salt and pepper to taste. Toss once more before covering pan with foil and placing in the oven.

Cook 25 minutes. Remove foil, toss vegetables and return to oven uncovered. Cook another 25 minutes until vegetables are tender.

Can be served hot as a side dish or cold as a salad.

CHAPTER

6

Pasta,
Grains & Beans

Teresa K. Toles' Creamy Macaroni & Cheese

Indianapolis, Indiana

SERVES 4

Source: Teresa Toles

As a little girl, Teresa Toles would not eat homemade macaroni and cheese, preferring the boxed stuff instead. It was not until she was in her late teens, watching her mother cook homemade macaroni and cheese, that she come up with her own way of cooking macaroni and cheese. "Now I have to cook macaroni and cheese for family and friends for holidays and events," she says. Special beneficiaries of "creamy mac" are members of Ms. Toles' church, where she is choir directress and president of various auxiliary groups.

2 teaspoons salt
6 cups water
1¾ cups elbow macaroni
3 cups milk
2 sticks butter or margarine, cut into pats
1 pound Colby cheese, crumbled
2 pounds Velveeta cheese, cut into pieces
2 cups shredded mild cheddar cheese

Preheat oven to 375° F.

Place water and salt in large pot and bring to a rapid boil. Add macaroni to boiling water, stir to separate, and let boil until tender (7–10 minutes). Drain in colander—do not rinse.

Pour noodles into a 9 x 12 baking dish. Dot the macaroni with the margarine. Mix well until all the margarine is melted and all the pasta is coated.

Stir in 1½ cups of the milk and add Colby cheese, mixing so it's evenly distributed. Stir in the Velveeta cheese and fold so it's evenly distributed. Next, add the cheddar cheese and stir well so it's evenly distributed.

Pour the remaining 1½ cups of milk over the macaroni mixture. Do not stir. Place in the oven and cook, uncovered, for 30 minutes or until the mixture begins to bubble.

Stir macaroni carefully, blending the milk with the cheese so all ingredients are evenly distributed. Bake 30–35 minutes more or until bubbly and lightly browned.

Denise Pines' Spaghetti Creole

Los Angeles, California

SERVES 6 TO 8

Source: Jeffrey Wright

Denise Pines is a marketing executive and competitive runner who often takes ribbing from her family and friends about her "lack" of cooking skills. The truth is, Ms. Pines' cooking skills are a well-kept secret. "I used to cook all the time with my mother until I became so good at it that it became my job to start dinner and then, eventually, cook the whole meal," she says. "I realized soon enough that if I did a poor job of it, I'd be released from my duty."

Since those school days, Ms. Pines hasn't ventured much into the kitchen, except to bake, a hobby she loves. There is one recipe, though, that has remained in her repertoire—to the delight of family and friends. "I learned this dish from my mom and have cooked it throughout my life. It's a go-to dish that people always seem to love."

3 to 4 small chicken sausages (microwave on high for 3½ minutes)
1 pound ground turkey
½ pound ground chicken
1 tablespoon mixed Italian herb seasoning
1 small white onion, chopped
3 stalks celery, chopped
½ green bell pepper, chopped
2 garlic cloves, chopped
1 pound medium shrimp, peeled and deveined
7 jumbo shrimp, peeled and deveined
2 cups mushroom marinara sauce
salt and pepper to taste
1 package spaghetti

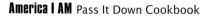

Microwave the chicken sausages for 3 minutes.

Heat olive oil in a large fry pan on medium heat. Add ground turkey and chicken, then add Italian herb seasonings. Fry 1–2 minutes.

While meats are still red, add onion, celery, bell pepper, and garlic. Fry 2–3 minutes or until the onion is softened.

Cut up cooked sausages and add them and shrimp to the pan. Mix well and cook until the shrimp just turns pink.

Using a slotted spoon, remove the meat mixture and place it in a clean, dry fry pan with the mushroom marinara sauce and ¼ cup of water. Simmer 10–15 minutes.

While the sauce is simmering, cook spaghetti according to package instructions and drain.

Place cooked spaghetti in a large platter, pour the meat and shrimp sauce over it, and serve.

Grandpa Peppermint's Speckled Butter Beans

Houston, Texas

SERVES 6 TO 8

"Growing up in Beaumont, Texas, in a large family of eight, my father always had a garden," writes LaLa Lewis. "In the summers he would grow butter beans, tomatoes, okra, onions, greens, and green beans. My favorite time was helping pick the butter beans and the whole family shelling them so that our mother could make a large pot of butter beans served with cornbread. As we grew older and moved away and had our own children, my father became known as Grandpa Peppermint, since he always had peppermints in his pocket, and my mother was Grandma Jelly Bean, since she always had jelly beans. My father continued with his garden until he passed away in 2003, but my mother, who is 88, taught me how to make my favorite Grandpa Peppermint's Speckled Butter Beans."

1 pound speckled butter beans
3 cups water
3 bacon slices, cut into small pieces
1 small onion, chopped
6 pieces of okra, cut into small slices
3 tomatoes, cut into pieces
2 teaspoons Creole seasoning (page 233)
1 tablespoon honey

Dried beans should always be soaked at a ratio of 3:1. One cup of dried beans should be soaked in 3 cups of cold water.

Shell butter beans and rinse well. Soak beans in water, 3:1 water to beans ratio.

While butter beans are soaking, heat a large cast iron pot and add the bacon pieces. When the bacon fat starts to render, add onion and okra. Fry until okra is slightly brown.

Add chopped tomatoes and Creole seasoning. Add 3 cups water and bring to a boil.

Drain the butter beans that have been soaking and place in boiling water.

Gently stir until water returns to a boil. Stir in tablespoon of honey, reduce the heat, cover and simmer 40–50 minutes until tender.

Pass It Down trick: *If you can't soak beans overnight to soften them, the next best thing is to bring them to a boil, simmer for 25 minutes, cover the lid and allow to soak for 1 hour. Then use as directed.*

··· The Peanut Doctor ···

George Washington Carver's Contributions to American Food

Source: Library of Congress

The Missouri-born child of a slave girl, George Washington Carver was destined to be different. When he was just one week old, he was kidnapped along with his mother and sister from their little home on the Diamond Grove, Missouri plantation of slaveowner Moses Carver. Only George was recovered by his master, trading a racehorse as ransom.

When slavery ended a year later, Moses Carver, a German immigrant, raised young George as one of his own children, teaching him to read and write, and pushing him toward a life of study, even though it meant relocating to a town ten miles away while still a little boy to attend a black school.

He moved to Kansas to attend high school and later college—which rejected him after admittance when, upon arrival, they saw he was an African American. But George persevered, working as a tenant farmer until he saved enough money to go to college in Indiana. In later years, his work on the farm growing subsistence crops would influence his work as a plant pathologist and mycologist. He specialized in crops that were easy to grow in poor soil, providing a living for the poorest of farmers, most of them African American.

George Washington Carver was touted as a new Renaissance man (he was called the "Black Leonardo" by *Time* magazine in 1941) because he was accomplished in music and art as well as science. But it was his scientific accomplishments that made him famous. He was interested not simply in crop research but how plants could provide relief from diseases like polio. He is most known for his work with peanuts at his laboratory at Tuskegee Institute in Alabama, where he created peanut products in the modern forms we know and use today, including peanut oil and peanut butter.

We think the following recipes from his 1916 work, *How to Grow the Peanut and 105 Ways of Preparing it for Human Consumption*, are a delicious testimony to Dr. Carver's talent and skill. They have been adapted slightly for use in the modern kitchen.

Peanut Salad Number Two

SERVES 4

The humble peanut becomes elevated in this simple salad that combines the legume with buttery Bibb lettuce, apples, and an easy Hollandaise-like sauce.

1 cup roasted peanuts, chopped roughly
1 large Granny Smith apple, peeled and sliced
½ cup water
½ cup sugar
2 tablespoons butter
½ cup vinegar
1 tablespoon flour
1 egg
1 head Boston Bibb lettuce, cleaned and trimmed

Mix the peanuts and apples together in a medium bowl. Set aside.

In a medium pot, whip together the water, sugar, butter, vinegar, flour, and egg. Place over medium-low heat, whisking constantly until the mixture thickens, about 3 to 4 minutes. Remove from heat and allow to cool to room temperature.

Layer a platter with the Boston Bibb lettuce leaves and sprinkle evenly with the peanut-apple mixture. Pour the dressing over the top of the salad. Serve immediately.

Did You Know? *Peanuts are not actually nuts at all. They are a legume—or a member of the bean family.*

Aunt Nellie's Peanut Brown Bread

MAKES 1 LOAF

George Washington Carver didn't indicate just who Aunt Nellie was, but, her flavorful take on simple brown bread is both tasty and healthy with extra protein from the wheat and peanut flours and limited fat.

1½ cups white flour
2 teaspoons baking powder
1½ cups whole wheat flour
1½ cups peanut flour
1–1½ teaspoons salt
2–2½ cups milk, or just enough to make a soft dough

Preheat oven to 350° F.

Sift the flours and salt together in a large bowl. Stir in the milk to make a thick batter.

Grease a loaf pan and pour in the batter. Bake for 1 hour or until a cake tester comes out clean.

Peanut Doughnuts Number Two

MAKES 12 TO 15 DONUTS

The ground peanuts add interesting texture to this donut recipe.

1 package yeast
2 cups milk
1 egg, well beaten
4 ounces butter (softened)
1 tablespoon lemon juice
1 cup sugar
5½–6 cups flour
2 cups peanuts, ground
2 cups or more canola oil

Dissolve the yeast and 1 teaspoon of sugar in ¼ cup of the milk, heated to 110° F.

When the yeast mixture is bubbly, mix it together with the remaining milk, egg, butter, lemon juice, and sugar. Slowly add the flour to form a sticky dough. Add the ground peanuts and mix well.

Place dough in a lightly oiled bowl covered with plastic wrap. Allow to rise 2 to 3 hours or until doubled in size.

Roll out dough on a well-floured board and cut out rounds using a 4-inch round cookie cutter or in squares, like beignets.

Add enough oil to a deep cast iron pot so that the depth of the oil is no more than ⅓ of the height of the pot. Heat until the oil reaches 350° F or a pinch of flour dropped into the oil bubbles vigorously. Carefully add the donuts, turning them once so that they are golden brown on both sides, about 1 minute per side. Remove the donuts from the oil and place on a wire rack set over a sheet tray or a paper-toweled-lined tray. Glaze with confectioners mixed with half & half, or sprinkle with confectioners sugar.

Serve warm.

Mock Veal Cutlets

SERVES 4

Vegetarians and meat eaters alike will appreciate this recipe for "mock" cutlets. For a vegan version, substitute soy yogurt for the egg prior to dredging.

1 cup lentils
¼ cup melted butter
2 cups bread crumbs
1 tablespoon minced celery
1 tablespoon minced onions
1 cup unsalted peanuts, ground to a coarse powder
1 cup tomato puree
⅛ teaspoon baking soda
1 teaspoon chopped parsley
½ teaspoon chopped thyme
¼ teaspoon salt
¼ teaspoon black pepper
1 egg, beaten with 2 tablespoons water

Rinse the lentils by placing in a bowl and covering with 2 cups of cold water. Swirl the lentils around in the water with your hand and gently pour off the water. Repeat, then add 2 cups clean cold water to the bowl and allow to soak over night.

Bring 2 cups of water to a boil and add the lentils. Boil until tender, about 20 minutes. Drain and place the lentils in a food processor and pulse into a puree.

Preheat the oven to 400° F. Make the cutlets: Add the butter, 1 cup of the bread crumbs, tomato puree and baking soda to the lentils and mix well. Add the peanuts, celery, onions, parsley, thyme, salt, and pepper. Mix thoroughly. The mixture should hold together enough to form into oblong patties about 4 inches long and 3 inches wide.

Dip the patties in the egg mixture and then bread both sides in the remaining bread crumbs. Grease a large baking dish with cooking spray such as Spectrum Natural Organic Oil Spray and layer the cutlets in the dish in one even layer. Bake until crispy, about 30 minutes. Serve with your favorite sides.

··· Bitter Grains ···

Source: Library of Congress

Rice was a high money crop. Slavers depended upon African labor to cash in on it. Slaves were integral to every part of the process, from planting to harvesting, drying, threshing, winnowing, and packaging it for sale. This 1867 engraving depicts the lifecycle of the rice industry—at every turn dependent on African American labor.

You can't have soul food in the Carolina low country or Louisiana if you don't have rice. As important as corn is to other parts of the South, rice is a reminder of West African heritage, where rice cultivation has taken place for more than 3,000 years. It was that knowledge that would not serve them well, as North American and European slavers came to their lands seeking labor for their rice fields. In fact, slaves from the "Rice Coast" regions—namely what is today Gambia and Sierra Leone—drew far higher prices because of their knowledge of rice growing.

Working a rice field was like working in a pit of stagnant water. Malaria was common, malnutrition was rampant, and most children didn't reach 16 years old. In many cases, the putrid conditions of South Carolina rice plantations drove white plantation owners to live elsewhere, leaving white foremen working along African "drivers" to run their estates.

The result was that African slaves on these plantations often retained their cultural ways more easily than slaves elsewhere in the country. This strong cultural tie to Africa is still seen among the Gullah/Geechee people (see Who Are the Gullah/Geechee? page 108).

Their backbreaking work created an industry that was highly prosperous for its owners. Just before the War for Independence, rice trade counted for more than half of all the South's exports. Even today, thanks to the industry built by the intelligence and sweat of African slaves, the United States ranks among the top five rice-producing and rice-exporting countries.

Pass It Down Classic Red Beans & Rice

New Orleans, Louisiana

SERVES 4 TO 6

Red beans and rice is a classic Creole New Orleans side dish that has its roots in a similar dish made in the Caribbean. In fact, red beans were brought to New Orleans directly from the West Indies.

3 tablespoons canola oil
1 large yellow onion, chopped small
3 ribs celery, white parts removed, chopped small
1 medium green bell pepper, chopped small
½ teaspoon salt
½ teaspoon black pepper
⅛ teaspoon cayenne pepper
3 bay leaves
2 tablespoons chopped flat-leaf parsley
2 teaspoons fresh thyme
1 pound andouille sausage, chopped
6 garlic cloves, minced
1 pound dried red (kidney) beans, soaked in 3 cups of water overnight, or two 15-ounce cans of kidney beans, rinsed
10 cups water
4 cups cooked white rice

Heat the oil in large pot over medium-high heat. Add the onions, celery, and bell peppers. Cook until soft.

Add salt, pepper, and cayenne. Cook, stirring until the vegetables are soft, about 3–5 minutes. Add bay leaves, parsley, thyme, and andouille sausage, stirring 3–4 minutes or until the sausage browns.

Add garlic and cook for 1 minute. Add beans and water, and bring to a boil. Reduce heat to simmer and cook uncovered, stirring occasionally, until beans are tender and start to thicken, about 2 hours (if beans dry out, add more water, about ¼ cup at a time). If you're using canned beans, simmer for just 40 minutes.

Using a slotted spoon, remove about 1 cup of the beans from the pot and place in a blender or food processor with ½ cup of the cooking water. Purée or pulse to achieve a smooth paste. Return the mashed beans to the pot and stir well. Cook 15 minutes more. Remove bay leaves and serve over rice.

Pass It Down Variation: Caribbean-Style Red Beans & Rice

Brooklyn, New York

SERVES 4 TO 6

Called peas and rice in the Caribbean, this dish has as many variations as there are islands in the West Indies. Kidney beans, black-eyed peas, or pigeon peas may be used. Coconut milk is a popular though unnecessary addition, and in some places salted pork is added. Sometimes the beans are served over rice and sometimes the rice is cooked with the beans. The Scotch bonnet pepper adds a kick the way cayenne pepper does in its Louisiana counterpart.

3 tablespoons canola oil

1 large yellow onion, chopped small

6 garlic cloves, minced

1 tablespoon green seasoning (page 232)

½ teaspoon salt

½ teaspoon black pepper

1 small Scotch bonnet (habañero) pepper

1 bay leaf

1 pound dried red (kidney) beans or pigeon peas (gandules), soaked in 3 cups of water overnight, or 2 15-ounce cans of kidney beans, rinsed

10 cups water

½ cup coconut milk

4 cups cooked white rice

Scotch bonnet or habañero peppers are the heart-shaped peppers richly hued in orange, deep red, and green. They are about 1 to 2 inches wide with a shiny, jewel-like skin—but don't be fooled this, little gem packs a big flavor—and heated—punch. Use it sparingly or you'll be sweating!

Heat canola oil in a large saucepan over medium-high heat and add onion. Cook until onion softens and becomes translucent. Add garlic and cook 1 minute more.

Stir in green seasoning, salt, black pepper, and Scotch bonnet pepper.

Add bay leaf and kidney beans or pigeon peas, and water. Stir well.

Add beans and water, and bring to a boil. Reduce heat to simmer and cook uncovered, stirring occasionally, until beans are tender and starting to thicken, about 2 hours. (If beans start to dry out, add more water, about ¼ cup at a time.) If you're using canned beans, simmer for just 40 minutes.

Remove Scotch bonnet pepper and add coconut milk. Simmer 15 minutes more. Serve over rice.

Kathleen Henry's Dirty Rice

Fenley, Nevada

SERVES 4 TO 6

Kathleen Henry says this recipe was taught to her by her husband and now it's her specialty. "He loves when I make it for him," she says.

2 tablespoons canola oil
1 pound ground beef
¼ teaspoon black pepper
½ teaspoon salt
½ onion, chopped small
½ green bell pepper, chopped small
½ red bell pepper, chopped small
3 celery stalks, white ends trimmed and chopped small
3 cups cooked white rice
1 teaspoon Mrs. Dash
1 teaspoon seasoning salt
1 teaspoon garlic powder
½ cup chicken stock (page 13)

Heat the oil on medium heat in a large pot. Add ground beef and fry until browned. Season with salt and pepper. Remove ground beef from pot with a slotted spoon and place in a bowl. Set aside.

Add the onion, green bell pepper, red bell pepper, and celery to the oil and fry until the celery is softened, 2–3 minutes. Remove vegetables with a slotted spoon and add to the cooked beef in the bowl.

Drain all but 1 tablespoon of oil from the pan. Return beef and cooked vegetables to the pan with the rice, Mrs. Dash, seasoning salt, and garlic powder. Mix well and add chicken stock.

Turn heat to low, place the lid on the pot, and cook for about 15 minutes, stirring often.

Angela Dodson's Hoppin' John

Trenton, New Jersey

SERVES 6 TO 8

Source: Astede Elegba

Food editor and writer Angela Dodson has a cookbook collection that numbers in the hundreds, and she credits her mixed Appalachian and Pennsylvania Dutch heritage, along with her husband Michael's Gullah/Geechee roots and Philadelphia heritage, for much of her cooking inspiration. "I have recorded about 28 years' worth of the menus for parties, holidays, and cookouts ever since we got married," she says. "I keep them in a journal along with recipes I have made up on the spot, and often with notations of which cookbook I've used or adapted them from. We have so much practice at giving parties and can entertain so spontaneously that friends joke that we could start "Michael and Angela's One-Hour Catering Service." Making Hoppin' John is a family tradition that needs no written recipe. It is served in Ms. Dodson's home, as in that of many African Americans, at New Year's for good luck. "We continue to serve—in some form—black-eyed peas, pork, and cabbage the first day of every year," she says.

1 1-pound bag of black-eyed peas
smoked turkey parts (1 wing part or a couple of pieces of neck bone)
1 medium-size whole Vidalia onion, chopped coarsely
3–5 cloves of garlic
2 or 3 stalks of celery with leaves, chopped
2 or 3 tablespoons sun-dried tomatoes, chopped
1 medium-size sweet red pepper, chopped
1 medium-size green pepper, chopped
3 sprigs thyme
1 teaspoon Italian seasoning
2 cloves
1-inch piece of rosemary
2 sage leaves
¼ teaspoon coriander seeds

2 teaspoons salt

⅓ teaspoon cayenne pepper

½ teaspoon black pepper

¼ cup brown sugar, maple syrup, or equivalent artificial sweetener

¼ cup vinegar, approximate

2 cups long grain rice

Soak beans overnight in large bowl with 6 cups cold water.

Bring 6 cups of water to a boil in a large stockpot. Drain beans and add them to the pot. Add onion, garlic, celery, sun-dried tomatoes, and red and green peppers.

Add the thyme sprigs, Italian seasoning, cloves, rosemary, sage, coriander, salt, black and red peppers, and mix well.

Stir in the sugar, syrup, or sweetener, and vinegar.

Simmer beans until they're soft, 2–3 hours. Add long-grain rice about 20 minutes before turning off the beans. Stir well and cook on low-medium heat. Adjust seasoning if necessary.

• •

Did you know? *Hoppin' John is descended from a dish that came from West Africa. A popular New Year's tradition in the coastal Southern states, versions of Hoppin' John can be found wherever there were once West African slaves, including the islands of the Caribbean.*

• •

Imani Wilson's Yellow Split Peas & Rice

Harlem, New York

SERVES 4 TO 6

"Aunt 'Dine, as my Bajan grandmother's eldest sister, Claudine, was known, held the title for the best version of this dish," says writer Imani Wilson. "Unlike the Jamaican rice and peas made with red kidney beans, or the Bajan (pigeon) peas and rice that made alternating appearances on our Sunday dinner table depending on which of my parents was on rice duty that week, split peas and rice was served on special occasions."

1½ cups yellow split peas
1 tablespoon vegetable oil
3 shallots, chopped
1 clove garlic, sliced
1–2 teaspoons yellow hot sauce
1½ teaspoons seasoning salt
1 tablespoon coconut cream
1½ cups basmati rice
½ teaspoon salt

Rinse and sort split peas to pick out any grown peas. Place 1 cup cold water and the rinsed split peas in a large saucepan and bring to a boil. Reduce heat and simmer for 20 minutes. Watch the pot—skim off and discard any foam that rises to the surface.

While peas are cooking, rinse the rice in three changes of water. In a large sauté pan, fry shallots and garlic over medium heat in vegetable oil until they begin to soften.

After 20 minutes, add fried shallots, garlic, seasoning salt, hot sauce, and coconut cream to peas. Cook until coconut cream melts. Add drained rice and 3 cups cold water and stir to mix.

Cover the pot, but not tightly so steam can escape. After 20 minutes, fluff the rice. Dissolve the sea salt in ⅓ cup cold water and add to rice and peas. Cook 5 minutes to finish.

Pass It Down Classic: Creamy Grits

Southern United States

SERVES 4

What is there to say about grits except everything? It came to us from Native Americans, who ground hominy on stone by hand. In Italy, they call it polenta. It has been the food of celebration, and the food that got folks through hard times when there was not much else to throw in the pot. Whether you like yours yellow or white, plain or cheesy, with butter or for breakfast, there's no denying that grits will always be one of the foods that feeds our soul.

3 cups chicken stock (page 13) or water
4 tablespoons butter
¼ teaspoon salt
1 cup quick-cooking white grits
1 cup heavy cream (optional)

In a large saucepan, bring the stock or water, butter, and salt to a boil.

Lower heat to a simmer and, using a wooden spoon, slowly stir in the grits, stirring the whole time.

Cook grits over low heat 15 minutes, stirring often. Remove from heat and stir in the heavy cream, if using. Serve with anything you'd serve with rice.

• •

Did you know? *Seventy-five percent of the grits sold in America are sold in what is known as the "grits belt," an area of the South from Virginia to Texas.*

• •

Robyn Frye's Cheesy Grits

Warwick, Rhode Island

SERVES 4

Cheesy grits are just as popular as plain grits in traditional Southern cooking. These are especially delicious with seafood.

4 cups water
¼ teaspoon salt
¼ stick butter
2 cups quick grits
¼ cup shredded mild cheddar cheese

In a medium saucepan, mix the water, salt, and butter, and bring to boil.

Add the grits and stir with a wooden spoon. Lower heat to low-medium and cook for 10 minutes, stirring often.

When grits are creamy and tender, about 10 minutes, add shredded cheddar cheese. Stir in the cheese until completely blended into grits. Serve as a side dish.

CHAPTER

7

Pass It Down
Menus

When planning a large gathering, menus are a good way to visualize the elements of the meal, making sure all the dishes complement each other and add interest to the celebration. A well thought out menu, with accompanying recipes, can help organize grocery shopping as well. By choosing a mix of dishes that can be prepared ahead or partially prepped, the cook can spend less time in the kitchen and more time at the party.

Party or Special Celebration Menu

This menu of small bites and little plates can easily be prepared ahead of your party so you can spend more time with your guests and less time in the kitchen. Everything is hand-held or easily portable to encourage sampling and mingling. Put out some pretty paper plates and you have less mess and less fuss when the soiree is over.

Leslie Forde's Grilled Shrimp Salad with Veggies (page 22)

CK's Brie in Puffed Pastry (page 27)

Mrs. Robinson's Spinach & Cheese Quiche (page 6)

Memphis Style BBQ Beef Tenderloin Sliders (page 271)

Rufus Estes' Corn Fritters (page 39)
with Justin Gillette's Cajun Remoulade Sauce (page 231)

Karilyn Park's World's Best Salmon Patties(page 117)

Saporous Strawberry Cheesecake (page 276)

Really Exciting Fruit Punch (page 249)

Easter Sunday Brunch Menu

Comforting, homey classics round out this post-church menu for Easter Sunday. While the recipes take a little extra time and care to prepare, you'll be more than rewarded by the appreciative thanks you'll get from your guests.

Mama and Mical's Pickled Eggs (page 269)

Peach-Glazed Easter Ham (page 89)

Dr. Carver's Sweet Potato Biscuits (page 46)

Calvetta McGill's Finger Lickin' Southern Fried Chicken (page 56)

Collard Greens with Smoked Pecans and Leeks (page 123)

Gillian Clark's Pineapple Upside Down Cake (page 202)

Sweet Tea (page 241)

Summer Picnic Menu

From the iconic deviled eggs to healthy, tasty sides like the Duo Dishes' Honey Dijon Spiced Pecan Slaw and Chef Jeff's Sautéed Succotash, and to traditional favorites like fried chicken and peach pie, this summer picnic menu has a little something for everyone.

Mom's Deviled Eggs (page 25)

The Duo Dishes' Honey Dijon Spiced Pecan Slaw (page 32)

Lillian Jackson's Fried Green Tomatoes (page 142)

Craig Robinson's Mom's Buttermilk Fried Chicken (page 54)

Chef Jeff's Sautéed Succotash (page 149)

Desmonette Hazly's Peach Pie (page 198)

Mint Julep—Kentucky Style (page 245)

Watermelon Iced Tea (page 242)

Sunday BBQ Menu

Barbecue may be a summer rite in the North, but in the South barbecue is an integral part of the culture year round. Regardless of where you live, you can enjoy barbecue at any time. The ribs can be prepared in the oven and the beans on the stovetop. Try it in the dead of winter to enliven dreary days with mouth-watering warmth of spice and smoke.

Ron Duprat's Jicama Slaw (page 24)

Mrs. Kathryn Brookshire's Bread & Butter Pickles (page 225)

Dwight Jones' St. Louis Style Ribs (page 91)

Soul Food Museum Southern Style Potato Salad (page 26)

Gillian Clark's Easy Corn Relish (page 133)

Patricia Lynch's Buttermilk Cornbread (page 42)

Chef Jeff's Red Velvet Cupcakes with Cream Cheese Icing (page 209)

Lemonade Apollinaris (page 244)

*'Cause I'm struttin' with some barbecue, feeling mighty grand,
pass another helping please, of that good ol' Dixie land.*
— Louis Armstrong, from "Struttin with Some Barbecue"

Anytime Ice Cream Social Menu

An ice cream social is a fun, all-generation inclusive way to get together without a day of cooking or the necessity for cocktails. Set out pretty bowls, cups, or even paperware to make it super simple. Brightly colored paper napkins can be cheerful too. We suggest sparkling water with a twist of lime as a refreshing accompaniment that doesn't add even more sugar to the mix.

Ice Cream Bon Bons
Vanilla Ice Cream (page 214)
Coconut Ice Cream (page 215)
Strawberry Ice Cream (page 214)
Butter Pecan Ice Cream (page 215)
Pistachio Ice Cream (page 215)
Chocolate Ice Cream (page 216)
Chocolate Cherry Ice Cream (page 216)

TOPPINGS
Coconut flakes
Fresh sliced strawberries
Fresh, pitted, sliced cherries
Chocolate chips
Peanut butter chips
Dried cranberries
Coarsely chopped almonds, cashews, and peanuts
Caramelly chocolate sauce (page 237)

Thanksgiving Dinner Menu

Not everyone likes turkey for Thanksgiving, and Russel Honoré's Barbequed Roast Boston Pork Butt offers high-flavored variety to the table. Traditional oyster dressing, macaroni and cheese, and butter beans share table space with new takes on old faves like collard greens and okra.

Donna Daniels' Sumac Roast Turkey (page 64)

Russel Honoré's Barbequed Roast Boston Pork Butt (page 93)

Four State Oyster Dressing (page 106)

Teresa K. Tole's Creamy Macaroni & Cheese (page 157)

Collard Greens with Smoked Pecans and Leeks (page 123)

Monticello Okra and Tomatoes (page 131)

Momma's Sweet Potato Pie (page 196)

Pomegranate Champagne Punch (page 248)

Did you know? *In Colonial times nearly twenty percent of the population of the thirteen colonies was of African descent. This included slaves and free people of color. Ironically, denied their own freedom, many African Americans still served valiantly alongside their white counterparts in the battle for American independence.*

Thanksgiving is an ideal time to raise a glass to these patriots, including Crispus Attucks, a leader in the anti-British protest that led to the Boston Massacre; Salem Poor, who served with commendation at the Battle of Bunker Hill; and Private Oliver Cromwell, who was with General George Washington at his famous crossing of the Delaware River on December 25, 1776.

Learn more about these men and others in the book African American Soldiers in the Revolutionary War *by Lucia Tarbox Raatma (Compass Point Books).*

©2009 Compass Point Books, a Capstone imprint

WE THE PEOPLE

African-American Soldiers in the Revolutionary War

by Lucia Raatma

Festive Winter Holiday Gathering Menu

Whether you celebrate Christmas, Kwanzaa, or are looking for a menu for a New Year's Day bash, the dishes in this menu make for a festive, stylish gathering. Traditional sides like black-eyed peas share the table with elegant nibbles like Justin Gillette's Low Country Crab Cakes and the Duo Dishes' Cornbread Panzanella, a soulful version of traditional Italian bread salad.

Duo Dishes' Cornbread Panzanella (page 33)

Gillette's Low Country Crab Cakes (page 4)

Eric Spigner's Everything In the Pot Gumbo (page 20)

Donna Daniels' Pork Chops with Shallots, Lemon, and Capers (page 87)

Ron Johnson's Crunchy Collards (page 124)

Angela Dodson's Hoppin' John (page 173)

Kathleen Henry's Dirty Rice (page 172)

Soul Food Museum Holiday Pecan Pie (page 217)

Pass It Down Georgia White Peach Sangria (page 247)

Pass It Down Classic Homemade Eggnog (page 251)

CHAPTER 8

Desserts

Momma's Bread Pudding

SERVES 6 TO 8

The beauty of bread pudding is that the basic recipe of bread, milk, eggs, and sugar can be the starting point for any number of variations. Chocolate, white chocolate, candied fruits, and even dried fruits can replace the pineapples, pecans, and coconut in Sandra Miller's version. Try multiple combinations—the possibilities are endless!

1 loaf French bread
4 cups milk, or more as needed
1 small can sweetened condensed milk
4 eggs
1 tablespoon vanilla extract
3 cups sugar
2 cups crushed pineapple
1 cup pecan pieces
1 cup shredded coconut
2 tablespoons cinnamon
1 tablespoon nutmeg
1 stick butter, melted

Preheat oven to 350° F. Slice the bread into cubes and place on a cookie sheet. Spray lightly with cooking spray and toast in the oven until lightly browned.

Place bread cubes in a large mixing bowl and crumble slightly with your hands. Add the milk slowly to help soften the bread. If needed, add more milk to ensure all the bread is saturated.

Beat the condensed milk, eggs, vanilla, and sugar together in another bowl. Using a spoon, add the mixture to the bread as well.

Stir in pineapple, pecans, coconut, cinnamon, and nutmeg, Add melted butter and mix well.

Pour pudding mixture into greased casserole dish and cover with tin foil. Place the dish in a large, deep tray or pot and fill the tray with water so it's about halfway up the side of the casserole dish.

Bake 45 minutes or until the bread pudding is puffed. Remove foil and cook 5–10 minutes more, or just until the top is lightly browned. Serve warm.

Mama Dip's Egg Custard Pie

Chapel Hill, North Carolina

SERVES 8

Source: UNC Chapil Hill Press

"I made my first Egg Custard Pie when I was nine years old," says Mildred Council, better known as Mama Dip. *"I would sit in the kitchen and watch as my older brother made meals, remembering everything he did. Papa asked me to fix food for lunch. I listened as the guinea cackled. Papa sold guinea eggs. I made a pie just like my brother. I never told Papa I used his guinea eggs to make the pie, but he said it was the best pie he ever ate."*

1 cup sugar

2 tablespoons self-rising flour

1 teaspoon nutmeg

¼ stick butter or margarine, melted

1 teaspoon vanilla extract

4 eggs, beaten

¼ cup milk

1 unbaked 9-inch pie shell

Preheat oven to 375° F.

In a bowl, mix sugar, flour, and nutmeg.

Stir in butter, vanilla, and eggs, and beat for 10 to 15 strokes. Add milk and mix well.

Pour into pie shell and bake 30 minutes or until firm.

"I have always known myself as Mildred Edna Cotton Council. The cultural names haven't changed my feelings of being an American citizen. I have experienced the Negro or black American cultural world in a tiny area of the United States of America. I grew up and lived in poverty most of my life without knowing it. My children, too, grew up in poverty, never knowing that they were poor. Our house just leaked. No screen doors. An outdoor bathroom and little money.

Our family was happy to sit around the table at dinnertime, eating, poking jokes, and having fun. It didn't matter if the dishes and the cups didn't match. (Sometimes just a pie pan would do.) Early childhood experience equipped me to raise my children to accept life by being happy, learning about life and its struggles and disappointments.

Desserts

Momma's Sweet Potato Pie

Newport News, Virginia

MAKES 4 PIES

Source: Abraham Brooks

Mrs. Jacquelyn Brooks is an honorably discharged military veteran with over 20 years of service. She has been married to her husband, Abraham, for nearly 50 years and has three children and two grandchildren. Hers is a life of faithful constants, and that includes making her grandmother's sweet potato pie for special occasions. "I often tease my mother about how I can make this pie better than she can, but the truth is I love being in the kitchen with my mother when she makes her sweet potato pies," she says. "I get an overwhelming feeling of comfort, love, and peace. It's the smell of homemade pies—there's nothing like it." Mrs. Brooks likes to have her sweet potato pie with butter pecan ice cream.

10 medium-size sweet potatoes
2½ sticks sweetened butter, softened
4 cups sugar
8 tablespoons cinnamon
4 eggs
2½ tablespoons nutmeg
2 cans Carnation evaporated milk
2½ tablespoons vanilla extract
4 9-inch frozen piecrusts

You can easily halve this recipe for only two pies, but Sweet Potato Pies freeze well. Prepare the pies as for baking, but cover well in tin foil or plastic wrap and freeze. Defrost in refrigerator one day before baking, then bake as usual.

Wash sweet potatoes. Place them in a large pot covered with 2 inches of water. Bring to a boil and reduce to a simmer. Have a large bowl ready with 2 cups of ice and 3 cups of water. Cook sweet potatoes until fork tender, then drain. Place the cooked sweet potatoes in the ice water 3–5 minutes. Remove from ice water, peel, and mash in a large bowl.

Place sweetened butter in the bowl of a stand mixer or use a large bowl with a hand mixer. Add the butter and 2 tablespoons of the cinnamon and blend well.

Add half of the sweet potato mash to the bowl and continue to blend while slowly adding 1 cup of the sugar. Mix well. When the mixture is thoroughly combined, add the remaining sweet potatoes, eggs, cinnamon, and nutmeg.

Slowly add evaporated milk and vanilla extract. Mix 2–3 minutes until batter is smooth and there are no lumps.

Pour the mixture equally between the 4 pie shells. Bake 1½ hours or until the tops are firm when jiggled. Allow pies to cool for 1 hour. Serve with whipped topping or ice cream.

Pass It Down variation: *Substitute ¾ cup of concentrated orange juice for every cup of white sugar and decrease the amount of liquid by three tablespoons. Although canned evaporated milk has the same vitamins and minerals as regular milk, it is high in sugar and can increase the risk for diabetes.*

Desmonette Hazly's Ginger Peach Pie

SERVES 10

Desmonette Hazly learned to cook from her grandmother who watched her and her cousins while their mothers worked. She often enlisted young Desmonette's help because of how much the child enjoyed being in the kitchen, hearing stories. Later, that love would prove to be a calling as she went on to be a chef and social worker using cooking as a way to outreach into struggling communities. Dr. Hazly's peach pie and peach pudding recipes are inspired by the bountiful peach trees that blessed her family yard when she was a child.

1 9-inch unbaked piecrust

FILLING

6 fresh, ripe peaches, peeled, pitted, and cut into ½-inch slices
1 teaspoon cinnamon
1 teaspoon nutmeg
½ teaspoon ginger
½ cup sugar
¼ cup flour
1 tablespoon vanilla extract
2 tablespoons butter, well chilled and cut into cubes

ALMOND CRUMBLE TOPPING

6 tablespoons butter, melted
⅓ cup brown sugar
⅓ cup white sugar
1 cup chopped almonds
½ cup flour
½ teaspoon cinnamon
½ teaspoon nutmeg
½ teaspoon ground ginger

Preheat oven to 450° F.

Make the filling by combining all ingredients. Place in pie shell.

Make the almond crumble topping by combining all ingredients. Mix well.

Top peaches with half of topping and bake at 450° F for 15 minutes. Reduce heat to 350° F and top pie with remainder of the crumb mixture. Bake an additional 30 minutes.

Serve warm with vanilla ice cream or whipped cream.

Sandra Chaisson's Mama's Homemade Pound Cake

Houston, Texas

MAKES 1 CAKE

Pound cake has been around for several hundred years and is so called because the original recipe called for one pound each of butter, sugar, flour, and eggs. It's lightness came from the air beaten into the batter. Some recipes call for a bit of baking powder. This one from Sandra Chaisson uses buttermilk, a natural leavening agent.

4 sticks butter, salted or unsalted
3 cups sugar, sifted once
6 large eggs
½ teaspoon salt
3 cups cake flour
½ cup buttermilk
1 tablespoon pure vanilla extract

Pre-heat oven to 325° F.

In a stand mixer, or large bowl using a hand mixer, cream butter and sugar together until light and fluffy.

Add eggs one at a time, making sure they're well combined after each addition.

Sift together cake flour and salt, and add slowly to butter and egg mixture.

Add buttermilk in a steady stream, adding more as needed to achieve a smooth thick batter. Stir in vanilla extract and stir until just combined.

Pour batter into a greased and floured Bundt cake pan. Bake 1 hour 20 minutes or until a cake tester inserted into the middle of the cake comes out clean.

Grandma Lillie's Vanilla Butternut Pound Cake

MAKES 1 CAKE

Source: Lisa Aikens

"My favorite memory of my Grandma Lillie's Vanilla Butternut Pound Cake is when I was a little girl and my grandmother used to be in her small row-house kitchen in Baltimore, Maryland. She would have her gospel music playing on the AM radio and have the back door to the kitchen open to let out the heat," says Lisa Aikens. "We weren't allowed in the kitchen when she was cooking the pound cake, but after she finished making the cake batter, Grandma would put some batter in small Dixie cups for me and my brother. She would write down the time she put the cake in the oven and exactly 1 hour and 45 minutes later my definition of cake perfection emerged."

2 sticks butter, softened
½ cup vegetable shortening
3 cups sugar
¼ teaspoon salt
5 large eggs
3 cups all-purpose flour
1 cup evaporated milk
2 tablespoons of vanilla butternut flavor

Pass It Down TIP

Baking enthusiasts looking for a non-imitation quality vanilla butternut extract can find it online at www.kingarthurflour.com/shop. Use less vanilla butternut if you are using a pure extract.

Place butter, shortening, sugar, and salt together in a stand mixer, or large bowl using a hand mixer. Cream until light and fluffy, about 4 minutes.

Add eggs one at a time, mixing until well incorporated after each addition.

Add 1 cup flour and mix until just combined. Add ⅓ cup evaporated milk to batter and mix well. Repeat, alternating flour and milk until they're completely added to the batter, ending with the flour.

Stir in vanilla butternut flavor by hand, pour into a greased Bundt pan, and place in a cold oven. Turn heat to 325º F and bake 1 hour 45 minutes or until a cake tester inserted into the center comes out clean.

Turn cake out onto a cake rack immediately when cake is done. Cool completely before serving.

Gillian Clark's Pineapple Upside-Down Cake

Washington, DC

MAKES 1 CAKE

Chef Gillian says she learned to cook from her father, who was, like her mother, born in Panama. "He was like a superhero in the kitchen to me," she says. "He was very adventurous with new recipes and yeast doughs. Sunday brunch was a big event at my house. We'd come back from Mass (we were Catholic) and Daddy would have this amazing brunch going. He'd make yeast doughs and all kinds of things. I was in awe of him. He made pineapple upside-down cake a lot."

TOPPING

½ cup butter
½ pound light brown sugar
¼ cup pineapple juice
6 canned pineapple rings
3 maraschino cherries, cut in half

CAKE

10 tablespoons butter
1 cup sugar
2 teaspoons pure vanilla extract
2 eggs
2 cups flour
½ teaspoons baking powder
½ cup pineapple juice
½ cup milk

MAKE THE TOPPING

Heat a 9 x 13 glass baking dish in the oven at 350° F.

Add butter to the warm dish. Remove dish from the oven when butter has melted and stir in brown sugar and pineapple juice.

Arrange pineapple rings in sugar mixture in two rows of three. Fill center of each ring with a cherry half. Set this aside to cool and set.

MAKE THE CAKE

In a stand mixer, cream butter and sugar. Add vanilla and eggs. In separate bowl, sift together flour, salt, and baking powder. Add butter and egg mixture to dry ingredients.

Stir in the pineapple juice and milk. Stir gently to form a lumpy but well-incorporated batter. Pour the batter over the topping in the dish. Bake in a 350° F oven for 35 minutes or until a toothpick pricked into the center of the cake comes out clean.

Cool for 5 minutes, and then invert the cake on a large cutting board or platter. Allow to cool 10 minutes more before cutting.

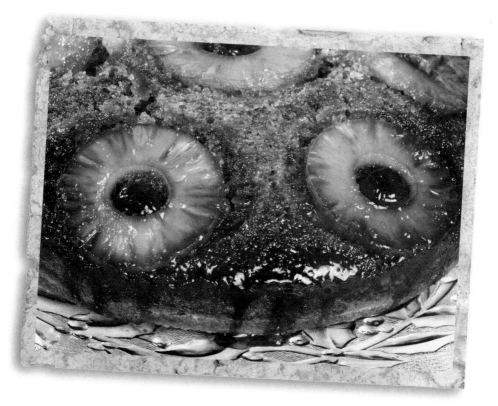

Dana Beck's Pineapple Cake

Benton Harbor, Michigan

MAKES 1 CAKE

Source: Dana Beck

Ms. Beck's niece Janay
loves pineapple cake.

More a quick bread than a cake, this easy recipe is perfect for a quick treat or easy-to-make company dessert. Dress it up a bit and complement the flavor of the pineapple by substituting a tropical nut, such as macadamia or cashew, for the walnuts.

2 cups sugar
2 eggs, beaten
2 cups flour
2 teaspoons baking soda
1 teaspoon vanilla extract
20 ounces crushed pineapples and juice (1 can)
½ cup chopped walnuts

FROSTING
1 8-ounce package cream cheese
1 stick margarine
1¾ cups powdered sugar

Preheat oven to 350° F.

In a large bowl, combine the sugar and eggs until creamy. Sift the flour and baking soda and add to the mixture, then add the pineapples and juice and vanilla extract. Mix well to achieve a smooth batter.

Stir in walnuts and pour mixture into a greased 9 x 12 x 2 pan. Bake at 350° F 35–40 minutes or until a cake tester inserted into the center of the cake comes out clean. Remove and cool on a cake rack.

While cake is baking make the frosting: Cream together the cream cheese and the margarine. Gradually add powdered sugar until light and fluffy. Spread on cake when cake is cooled.

Did you know? *Guar gum is a natural edible thickening agent extracted from the guar bean. Most gluten-free flour recipes add a binder like guar gum or xanthan gum for wheat-free to properly bind the mixture.*

The Traveling Cupcake's 3-Layer German Chocolate Cake

Brooklyn, New York & Jackson, New Jersey

SERVES 14

Donna Hicks-Izzard, left, and Jacqui Powell,
co-owners of The Traveling Cupcake

This recipe for German chocolate cake was passed down to Donna Hicks-Izzard from her mother Inez. Hicks-Izzard says after she started baking for her church and friends, she received a vision from God to continue her family legacy by starting a bakery business. With the help of her partner, Jacqui Powell, "The Traveling Cupcake" was launched. Each cake from The Traveling Cupcake starts with a prayer and travels with love as they are shipped all over the country.

GERMAN CHOCOLATE CAKE

4 ounces sweet dark chocolate

2¼ cups cake flour

¾ cup unsweetened cocoa powder

1½ teaspoons baking powder

½ teaspoon baking soda

½ teaspoon salt

1 cup boiling water

1 cup buttermilk

1¼ cups unsalted butter, softened

2½ cups granulated white sugar

5 large eggs

1½ teaspoons pure vanilla extract

Pass
It Down
TIP

When you have something great to offer, start a business. I did!

Preheat oven to 350° F and place rack in center of oven. Spray three 8-inch round baking pans with vegetable spray with flour and then line with parchment paper.

Place small pot over a saucepan of simmering water and melt the chocolate.

Once chocolate is melted, let cool to room temperature.

In a separate bowl, sift cake flour, cocoa powder, baking powder, baking soda, and salt. Set aside for later.

In a small bowl, combine hot water and buttermilk. In another mixing bowl, add butter and sugar and beat for about 5 minutes, then add the eggs one at a time.

Add the vanilla extract and beat again. Now add the buttermilk mixture to the cake flour mixture and beat well, then add the melted chocolate (this completes your cake batter).

Divide the batter evenly among three pans and bake for about 30–35 minutes. Cool cakes completely before frosting.

COCONUT-PECAN FROSTING

1½ cups pecans
1 cup heavy cream
1 cup granulated white sugar
4 large egg yolks, lightly beaten
½ cup unsalted butter
1/8 teaspoon salt
2 cups sweetened flaked coconut
½ teaspoon pure vanilla extract

Preheat the oven to 350° F. Place pecans on a baking sheet and roast for 10 minutes. Cool, then chop.

In a saucepan, combine heavy cream, sugar, egg yolks, butter, and salt. Cook over medium heat and stir constantly until mixture boils and thicken. Remove from heat and stir in the pecans, coconut, and vanilla extract.

TO ASSEMBLE THE CAKE

Take the first layer and place on your cake plate. Cover entire layer with frosting. Place second layer of cake on top of the first layer and frost with additional frosting. Now add the third layer and complete frosting of cake.

Optional: Garnish with additional pecans on top of cake.

Pass It Down variation: *Substitute 1 cup of buttermilk with 1 cup of sour cream. To enhance chocolate flavor, use hot coffee instead of hot water.*

JUST DESSERTS

Many years ago when I got into the culinary arts, I tried my hand at baking because I love sweets, especially cookies, pound cakes, German chocolate cake, peach cobbler, and red velvet cake. My grandmother was the only person around me and my sister Junell who had a cookie jar, and of course I was always in it. My granddaddy was a janitor at several bakeries in the Wilshire district in Beverly Hills, and he always used to bring home sweets. He knew how to make desserts too though, including bread pudding. He didn't use a recipe. My granddaddy just took the left over raisin bread and got some milk, eggs, butter, sugar, nutmeg, cinnamon, and a little caramel, and put it in the baking dish. Before you knew it, we had an excellent dessert. That dish and many others instilled the joy of baking in my soul.

In order to complete a truly great meal, especially in the African American community, you have to finish it off with a remarkable dessert. You know, it's that one piece of sweet dessert that will put you to sleep and take you over the top at the end of the day—whether it's a scoop of vanilla ice cream with some sautéed peaches or a slice of pound cake.

— CHEF JEFF

Chef Jeff's Red Velvet Cupcakes with Cream Cheese Icing

Las Vegas, Nevada

MAKES 12 TO 16 CUPCAKES

Red velvet cake has been a very popular dessert in the South for a long time. There's a lot of controversy on how to make it best. Chef Jeff, who always wanted to be a baker, likes to keep it simple, using classic ingredients and just a bit of extra sugar. His family likes it sweet.

2 cups all purpose flour
1½ teaspoons baking soda
pinch of salt
1 cup buttermilk
2 large eggs
1½ teaspoons vanilla extract
1 tablespoon white vinegar
2 tablespoons cocoa powder
3 tablespoons red food coloring
1 stick unsalted butter, softened
1½–2 cups granulated sugar

CREAM CHEESE ICING

1 stick unsalted butter, softened
1½–2 cups powdered confectioner's sugar
½ pinch salt
8 ounces cream cheese, softened
1 teaspoon vanilla extract

CUPCAKES

Preheat oven to 350° F. In a medium bowl, whisk flour, baking soda, and salt, and set aside. In a separate medium bowl, whisk buttermilk, eggs, vanilla, and white vinegar, and set aside. In a small bowl, whisk cocoa powder and food color until it becomes a paste.

With a table top or hand-held mixer in a large bowl, beat the softened butter and sugar on medium speed until fluffy, about 2 minutes. Scrape down sides of bowl, then beat 30 seconds to 1 minute. Add half of flour mixture and beat on low speed about 45 seconds until incorporated, then add half the buttermilk mixture and beat until combined. Repeat, adding remaining flour mixture, then remaining buttermilk mixture. Beat until thoroughly incorporated.

Line cupcake pans with paper cup cake liners. Spoon batter into paper liners until ¾ full. Place pans in oven on center rack. Bake cupcakes until a toothpick inserted in the center comes out clean, 22–25 minutes. Remove pans from oven and let cool at room temperature.

ICING

Using tabletop or a hand-held mixer, add all ingredients. Beat on medium-high until mixture is fluffy, about 3 minutes, scraping bowl as needed. Refrigerate until ready to use.

ASSEMBLY

After cupcakes have cooled, remove cream cheese icing from refrigerator. Using pastry spatula or butter knife, spread desired amount of icing on each cupcake.

• •

Did you know? *Stevia is a popular sugar substitute that contains many health benefits, especially for those who are insulin-intolerant or diabetic.*

1 Tsp Stevia (powered)=1 Cup Sugar

1 Tsp Stevia (liquid)=1 Cup Sugar

½ Tsp Stevia=1 Tbsp Sugar

6 Drops Liquid Stevia=1 Tbsp Sugar

A Pinch of Stevia=1 Tsp Sugar

2 Drops Liquid Stevia=1 Tsp Sugar

• •

Mama Mabel's Apple Dumplings

Atlantic City, New Jersey

MAKES 6 LARGE APPLE DUMPLINGS

Michele Washington, a designer who lives in New York City, remembers having apple dumplings at Philadelphia's Wannamaker's Department store on a day trip from Atlantic City, where she was raised. Cutting into the flaky crust, she took a bite—and nearly spit it out. "I told you they wouldn't be like your grandmother's," her mother admonished her. Unlike Ms. Washington's grandmother Mabel Hamilton's dumplings, the Wannamaker version—like most—was simply a crust enveloping a whole apple that had been cored and had sugar with spices packed into the hollow. "My grandmother always used sliced apples and sweet crust and the apples were seasoned delicately and evenly," says Ms. Washington. "I remember watching her make them, my head barely reaching the counter. Her dumplings were precious to me, like my very own small personal apples pies. Mabel was my grandmother's name, but my mother, her brother, my own brothers and I all called her Mama."

FOR DOUGH

3 cups all-purpose flour
5 tablespoons sugar
½ teaspoon salt
2 sticks cold unsalted butter, cut into small cubes
2 large egg yolks
3 tablespoons ice water or more as needed

FOR FILLING

6 large Granny Smith apples, peeled, cored, and sliced
¾ cup of turbinado or light brown sugar
1 teaspoon cinnamon
1 teaspoon of whole nutmeg grated
½ teaspoon of mace
6 pats butter

MAKE THE DOUGH

Sift together flour, sugar, and salt and place in a large bowl.

Using your fingertips or a pastry cutter, cut in the butter until you have a coarse meal with pea-sized clumps.

Beat the yolks and water together in a small bowl and stir them into the flour mixture until well combined. Add more ice water, 1 teaspoon at a time, as needed, to form a rough dough.

Flour a board or work surface and turn the dough out. Sprinkle dough surface with flour and knead lightly until it is combined. This is only 5 or 6 kneads. Do not overwork dough.

Form the dough in two balls, and then flatten into disks. Wrap with plastic wrap and refrigerate for at least 1 hour and up to 2 days.

Place the apples in a large mixing bowl. In a smaller bowl, combine the cinnamon, grated nutmeg, mace, and turbinado sugar, and then sprinkle this mixture over the sliced apples in the bowl. Mix well to make sure the apple slices are all coated.

Set aside and cover the bowl with a damp paper towel or kitchen dish towel.

Remove the dough from the refrigerator and let sit for 10 minutes on the counter. Divide each dough disc into 3 equal sections.

Working with one piece of dough at a time, place the dough on a floured piece of wax paper. Flour the dough surface and place another piece of wax paper on top of it. Press down on the wax paper with the palm of your hand to flatten the dough between the two pieces.

Using a rolling pin, roll over the dough to smoothly flatten into squares, roughly 8 inches by 8 inches.

Divide the apple filling into 6 equal portions and place one portion in the middle of dough squares. Place 1 pat of butter on top. Apply egg wash to all of the edges, then fold up edges neatly and pinch together to form a pouch. Repeat until all the dough and all the filling is used up. You will have 6 dumplings.

Place the dumplings on a cookie sheet lined with parchment paper and place in the refrigerator for 15 minutes.

Preheat oven to 375° F. Remove dumplings from the refrigerator and brush with milk. Bake for 45 minutes or until the crust is a golden brown. Remove from oven and cool 1 hour before serving.

··· The Ice Cream King ···

Augustus Jackson and America's Favorite Treat

Source: Library of Congress

Augustus Jackson was one of the many African American chefs who produced delicacies in the White House kitchen. In 1820, when James Monroe was president, he left that position to forge out on his own in Philadelphia as an ice cream maker. Ice cream was a popular confection that Jackson would have certainly produced often during his tenure at the White House—though he did not invent it. Already popular in European courts, dignitaries from Thomas Jefferson to James Madison served ice cream at political events. Augustus Jackson's contribution to ice cream really came with the new flavors he packaged in tin cans and delivered to the new and growing ice cream parlors around the city—helping to ensure that ice cream became a must-have American treat.

Vanilla Ice Cream

MAKES 2 QUARTS

Basic vanilla ice cream, thickened with the use of gelatin for lightness, makes a great starting point for fruit ice creams as well.

1 packet gelatin powder
2 cups whole milk
2 cups heavy cream
1 cup sugar
1 teaspoon vanilla extract or 1 whole vanilla bean

You can make virtually any ice cream from virtually any fruit, as long as it is not so acidic as to curdle the ice cream base. Simply add 1 cup of the desired fruit, chopped, in the last 5-10 minutes of churning. Chopped nuts make lovely additions as well.

Dissolve the gelatin powder in ¼ cup of whole milk and set aside.

Heat the remaining whole milk, heavy cream, and sugar in large saucepan. Add vanilla extract, or split the vanilla bean, if using, down its length. Using a paring knife, scrape out seeds and add to the milk mixture.

Heat milk mixture on medium heat to just under a boil (scald). Stir constantly to dissolve sugar and ensure mixture does not boil.

Add bloomed gelatin mixture to the heated milk. Using a whisk, make sure it's dissolved and well incorporated.

Remove mixture from heat and cool completely in refrigerator or by placing the mixture in another heat-safe bowl that can be set over an ice water bath in a larger bowl.

When mixture is completely chilled, pour into an ice cream maker and churn according to manufacturer's instructions.

Chill ice cream in a freezer-safe container for at least 8 hours before eating.

Pass It Down Variations

Peach: Add 1 cup fresh peaches, peeled and chopped into small pieces, or 1 cup frozen, peeled, sliced peaches in last 5 minutes of churning.

Strawberry: Add 1 cup fresh, hulled strawberries, chopped into small pieces, or 1 cup frozen, peeled, sliced strawberries in last 5 minutes of churning.

Coconut: Substitute 2 cups coconut milk for regular milk in the vanilla ice cream recipe and add ½ cup grated (unsweetened) coconut, fresh or dried, to mixture before churning.

Butter Pecan: Add 2 cups of finely chopped, oven-toasted pecans in the last 5 minutes of churning.

Pistachio: Add 1 cup unsalted, shelled pistachios to mixture in last 5 minutes of churning.

• •

Did you know? *Vanilla is actually a type of orchid. The bean is actually the fruit of the plant and, when green, resembles a string bean on the plant.*

• •

Pass It Down TIP

Reuse vanilla beans after the seeds have been scraped away by placing the pods in a jar of sugar, for tasty vanilla sugar to sweeten hot drinks.

Chocolate Ice Cream

Who doesn't love chocolate ice cream? This basic recipe can be tweaked and made special by the addition of anything from coconut flakes to dried fruit.

1 packet gelatin powder
2 cups whole milk
2 cups heavy cream
1 cup sugar
½ cup unsweetened cocoa powder

Dissolve the gelatin powder in ¼ cup of whole milk and set aside.

Heat remaining whole milk, heavy cream, sugar, and cocoa powder in large saucepan.

Heat milk mixture on medium heat to just under a boil (scald). Stir constantly to dissolve sugar and ensure mixture does not boil.

Add bloomed gelatin mixture to heated milk. Using a whisk, make sure it's dissolved and well incorporated.

Remove mixture from heat and cool completely in the refrigerator or by placing mixture in another heat-safe bowl that can be set over an ice water bath in a larger bowl.

When mixture is completely chilled, pour into an ice cream maker and churn according to manufacturer's instructions.

Chill ice cream in a freezer-safe container for at least 8 hours before eating.

Pass It Down Variations

Chocolate Chocolate Chunk: Add ½ cup chopped semisweet chocolate or chocolate chips to mixture before churning.

Chocolate Peanut Butter Chip: Add ½ cup peanut butter chips to mixture before churning.

Chocolate Cherry: Add ½ cup fresh, pitted cherries, chopped into small pieces or 1 cup frozen pitted cherries, in last 5 minutes of churning. For an extra twist, use ½ cup dried cherries soaked in 3 tablespoons hot water and 1 tablespoon rum or brandy. When cherries have plumped, about 15 minutes, drain liquid and press gently on cherries to squeeze out any excess liquid. Add to ice cream in last 5 minutes of churning.

Soul Food Museum Holiday Pecan Pie

Atlanta, Georgia

SERVES 8

Source: Kenneth Willhoite

"This recipe is always a family favorite at the dinner table and is made with a lot of love," says Dr. Willhoite. "Adding whipped cream and fresh mint adds a special touch to the Soul Food Museum Holiday Pecan Pie."

The Soul Food Museum will hit the road soon showcasing its unique collection of African American food products, cooking memorabilia, and gallery of famous chefs and restaurateurs in a 1,000-square-foot double-wide truck. This brainchild of Dr. Willhoite and DeAndrea Reynolds will tour 47 states and visit Black expos, festivals, conferences, and HBCUs.

3 eggs
1 cup brown sugar
1 teaspoon all-purpose flour
1 cup corn syrup
1 teaspoon salt
2 tablespoons butter, melted and cooled (I prefer Land-O-Lakes butter)
1½ teaspoons vanilla extract
1½ cups fresh pecans
1 9-inch unbaked pie shell

Pre-heat oven to 350° F.

Gently beat eggs in a medium bowl. Stir in sugar and flour and then add the syrup, salt, butter, and vanilla extract. Fold in pecans.

Pour mixture into the pie shell. Bake for 50–60 minutes or until a knife inserted comes out clean. Add whip cream once the pie has cooled and serve at room temperature. Garnish with fresh mint and enjoy.

Fabulous Fruit Frappe

MAKES FOUR 6-OUNCE SERVINGS

Whether you call it a frosty, shake, smoothie, or frappe, it's a smooth and chilly treat. For a taste that's all your own be creative with the types of fruit, or fruit mixes, that you use as well as the ice cream flavor.

1 cup fresh fruit
1 pint vanilla ice cream

Place fruit in blender and pulse until you achieve a thick purée, 1–3 minutes, depending on the kind of fruit.

Add ice cream and pulse quickly for 5–10 seconds or until just combined. Don't pulse too much or the ice cream will become liquid.

Serve in tall glasses with a straw.

• •

Pass It Down variation: *Substitute 1 pint of low-fat frozen yogurt. Yogurt is enjoying renewed popularity because many brands are low-fat and contain healthy bacteria.*

• •

Ambrosia or Five-Cup Salad

Trenton, New Jersey

SERVES 4 TO 6

"I am not sure where this recipe originated, but I have a vague recollection that it might have been passed on to my mother at a Dodson-Hairston reunion as early as the 1960s in Charleston, West Virginia or Columbus, Ohio," writes Angela Dodson of her Ambrosia or "5-cup salad," so named for the 1 cup of each of its five ingredients.

In fact, the name of the dish is often a source of debate among Ms. Dodson's friends. "I have seen it or variations of it in cookbooks, but have never seen anyone else serve it. It appears to be linked to Appalachian cooking, centered in West Virginia, southern Ohio, and Kentucky," she says. "I learned to make it from the time I was about 12, and was designated to prepare it for holidays. I taught it to my four sons when they were little (now adults), and it is considered a requirement for winter holiday dinners, especially Thanksgiving, Christmas, and other gatherings. It is best made ahead of time and left to sit a few hours or overnight so the marshmallows can absorb the juices and plump up."

1 cup (8 ounces) canned mandarin oranges
1 cup (8 ounces) canned pineapple
1 cup (8 ounces) sour cream
1 cup shredded coconut
1 cup small marshmallows

Drain the canned oranges and pineapple and place them in a large bowl.

Fold in the sour cream, coconut, and marshmallows.

Chill before serving. It can be made a day ahead and is best when chilled for at least two hours. It also keeps a couple of days, properly refrigerated.

• •

Pass It Down Variation: *Angela Dodson says she has found variations in cookbooks for 6-Cup Salad and 7-Cup Salad, and so on by adding 1 cup of nuts, such as walnuts, pecans, or almonds, and 1 cup maraschino cherries. If you use cherries, she says to drain them well and add just before serving, or the whole salad will turn pink.*

• •

Barbadian Coconut Flapjacks

Washington, DC

MAKES 8 TO 12

Marguerite Pridgen's grandparents came to the United States from Barbados in the early 1900s, settling in Cambridge, Massachusetts. Barbadian (or Bajan) style cooking was a way for them to pass down their West Indian pride to their children. "My mother told me stories about how, when she was a child, neighbors would visit their home just for a taste of my grandmother's cuckoo or rice and peas. My grandfather became known for his baked breads, pastries, and other sweets," she says.

"One of the baked dishes my mother fondly remembers is her father's coconut flapjacks—which are not like pancakes at all—they are more like oat cookie bars with coconut," Ms. Pridgen says. "Her father would bake these special treats when he had some rare spare time, and the smell would permeate the multifamily house. To this day, if you mention her father and coconut flapjacks in the same sentence, she smiles and recounts the taste of her childhood."

2 cups rolled outs
1 cup desiccated (unsweetened) coconut
½ teaspoon salt
½ cup sugar
4 tablespoons brown sugar
5 tablespoons butter
4 tablespoons golden syrup (or mix 2 tablespoons light corn syrup,
    1 tablespoon molasses, or 1 tablespoon honey)

Preheat oven to 350º F. Grease an 8 x 8 baking pan and set aside.

Put the oats, coconut, salt, and sugars into a bowl and mix well.

Place butter in a small saucepan, add golden syrup, and warm on very low heat until syrup slides right off a wooden spoon.

When butter mixture is ready, pour over oats and mix well. Press mixture into the buttered baking dish and smooth the top. Score into 8 to 12 rectangles.

Bake 15–20 minutes or until lightly browned. Cool 5 minutes and cut along score lines.

9

Extras

Pickles, Condiments, Spices & Sauces

Mrs. Kathryn Brookshire's Bread & Butter Pickles

Atlanta, Georgia

MAKES 12 PINT JARS

Why these pickled cucumbers are called "bread and butter" no one is quite sure. Some sources say that they were so cheap and easy to prepare they became a staple on Depression-era tables— just like bread and butter. Whatever the origin of the name, these pickles are tasty at picnics, with a sandwich, or just as a condiment with supper.

5 pounds Kirby cucumbers
8 medium onions
½ cup salt
5 cups sugar
5 cups vinegar
1 tablespoon mustard seed
1 teaspoon turmeric powder
1 teaspoon whole cloves

Slice the cucumbers and onions into ¼ inch slices.

Place the cucumbers and onions in a large bowl and add salt. Add just enough cold water to cover. Soak for 3 hours.

Bring the sugar, vinegar, mustard seed, turmeric, and clove to a boil in a large stock pot. Add the cucumbers and onions. Bring back to a boil

Pack the pickles in mason jars with their pickling liquid and seal tightly. Process the jars in a boiling water bath canner for 10 minutes. Remove the jars and allow them to cool.

Lula Momma's Chow Chow

St. Louis, Missouri

MAKES 20 PINTS PICKLES

Source: Felicia Pearson

When folks put up pickles they don't do it in small batches. Felicia Pearson remembers her grandmother making this recipe and giving it out as gifts to her family and friends. "I give you this recipe in dedication to my Lula Momma," she says. "I remember everyone looking forward to this special treat to put on greens, sandwiches, and various other vegetables."

4 quarts green tomatoes, cut into large pieces
1 large cabbage, cored and shredded
10 medium white onions, chopped
4 cucumbers, washed and sliced
5 green bell peppers, chopped
3 red bell peppers, chopped
2 orange bell peppers, chopped
2 yellow bell peppers, chopped
1½ tablespoon salt
15 gallons white vinegar
5 cups sugar
3 tablespoons dry mustard
1 teaspoon powdered ginger
1 tablespoon turmeric
1 tablespoon paprika
4 tablespoons mustard seeds
4 tablespoons celery seed
1 tablespoon pickling spice
3 red chili peppers
6-inch square of cheese cloth or cheesecloth bag

In large stockpot, mix green tomatoes, cabbage, onions, cucumbers, green peppers, red bell peppers, orange peppers, and salt. Mix well and let stand at room temperature overnight or at least 8 hours. Drain and set aside.

Combine vinegar, sugar, dry mustard, ginger, turmeric, and paprika in large pot. Put mustard seed, celery seed, and pickling spices in a 6-inch square of cheesecloth or cheesecloth bag. Tie ends and add to the pot. Add chili peppers to the pot.

Bring liquid to a boil and simmer 30 minutes. Add vegetables and return to simmer for 30 minutes more. Discard spice bag and spoon chow chow into hot, sterilized jars and seal according to manufacturer's directions (see Tips for Boiling Water Bath Canning, page 228).

Store in cool, dry place for at least 3 weeks before serving.

··· Tips for Boiling Water Bath Canning ···

from PickYourOwn.org

These tips on home canning, reprinted courtesy of Pick Your Own, are a good primer on canning your own fresh vegetables or making pickles. Most canners come with very good instructions, and it's important to follow these carefully to ensure safety both when canning and when eating your final product.

Find more tips on pickling, canning, and preserving at **www.pickyourown.org**.

• • •

Fill canner at least halfway with water. A little practice will help you to know how much water you'll need to start out with to ensure the jars will be covered by at least 1 inch of water.

Preheat water that's added to the jars (when called for) to very warm but not boiling (around 140º F.) for raw-packed foods (the lower temperature helps to reduce jar breakage) and to boiling for hot-packed foods.

Put the filled jars, with lids and rings on, onto the canner rack and use the handles to lower the rack into the water. Or you may fill the canner, one jar at a time, with a jar lifter. Obviously, you'd need to be quick, or the first jar could be in the bath for substantially longer than the last jar you add. If you don't use a jar rack, then a flat rack on the bottom helps to reduce breakage. One of these comes with each canner.

Always add more boiling water, if needed, so the water level is at least one inch above the tops of the jars.

Turn heat to its highest position until the water boils vigorously, and then set a timer for the minutes required for processing the food.

Cover the canner and, if necessary, lower the heat setting to maintain a full but gentle boil throughout the processing time. Generally, I find I need to keep the burners on high.

If one burner doesn't produce enough heat to keep the water boiling, you can usually straddle two burners with the canner.

When the jars have been boiled for the recommended time, turn the heat off and use a jar lifter to remove the jars and place them on a towel in an area that is not drafty, leaving at least one inch between the jars during cooling.

Do not retighten the jar lids—it may break the seal.

Do not leave the jars in the boiling water after processing time is done, because the food will become overcooked.

Check the jar seals 12–24 hours after processing for leaks and broken seals. Just press down on the lid. If it's sealed, it will be sucked down tight. If it did not seal, it will flex and make a popping sound each tip.

To store, remove the screw bands and wipe the jars clean. Otherwise, the rings may rust tight to the jar!

If any jar fails to seal, the contents can be reprocessed in a clean jar with a new lid. Reprocess within 24 hours. Generally, it's better to refrigerate the jar and use it within several days. The jar may also be stored in the freezer if the headspace is adjusted to 1½ inches to allow for expansion of the product.

Janice Gairy's Pickled Beets

Minneapolis, Minnesota

Source: Janice Gairy

Janice Gairy is a food photo stylist who works with food daily, but that doesn't dampen her enthusiasm for cooking meals at home. She remembers growing up in Mansfield and Dayton, Ohio and watching her grandmother make every single meal from scratch, rising before dawn to make her grandfather's breakfast of homemade biscuit with sorghum, scrambled eggs, or ham with red-eye gravy. Her favorite thing to do was to pull taffy out on the cold back porch, using the hot corn syrup her grandmother made. Her pickled beet recipe isn't as complex as those dishes she learned at her grandmother's knee, but it's just as tasty.

2½ cups cooked or canned beets, sliced, juice reserved
1 small onion, sliced thinly
1 teaspoon horseradish
½ green bell pepper, seeded and sliced
½ cup white vinegar
2 tablespoons sugar
6 cloves
½ teaspoon salt
5 peppercorns
2 bay leaves

Place beets in a heat-proof, medium-size bowl with onion, horseradish, and bell pepper. Mix well and set aside.

In a medium saucepan, add white vinegar, sugar, cloves, salt, peppercorns, and bay leaves, and bring to a boil. Reduce to a simmer and cook 5 minutes. Remove from heat and strain.

Pour hot, strained beet juice mixture over beets and vegetables. Allow to cool and refrigerate. Serve cold as a side dish.

Justin Gillette's Cajun Remoulade

Atlanta, Georgia

Although Justin Gillette uses this remoulade to accompany his crab cakes, it's a good accompaniment for anything from sandwiches to French fries.

¼ cup of mayonnaise
2 teaspoons Cajun seasoning (name brand or generic)
1 fresh squeezed lime
¼ bunch cilantro, chopped

In a mixing bowl, combine all ingredients and mix well.

When well incorporated, serve atop or alongside the crab cakes.

To spice it up more, add 2 teaspoons of Tabasco.

Green Seasoning

Queens, New York

Green seasoning is a common spice paste in the Caribbean, where it's used primarily for meat and fish. The exact mixture and quantity of spices varies island to island and also according to the cook's taste. Experiment with your own measurements to find what you really like. This is Imani Wilson's family recipe.

1 bunch parsley
1 bunch thyme
1 bunch chives
1 bunch scallions
1 bunch cilantro
1 bunch cutting celery
1 bunch shado beni or culantro
5 shallots, sliced
3 garlic cloves, sliced
1 tablespoon sea salt
1 tablespoon black pepper

Wash all herbs and dry them in a salad spinner. If thyme stems are woody, remove leaves and discard stems.

Chop parsley, chives, scallions, cilantro, celery, and shado beni coarsely. Place all ingredients in bowl of food processor with ½ cup water and process to a rough paste. Herbs should not become liquefied.

If necessary, continue to add up to ½ cup of water, 1 tablespoon at a time, to facilitate processing. Refrigerate for up to 1 week.

"There is a communication of more than our bodies when bread is broken and wine is drunk."

— **MFK Fisher**

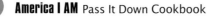

Pass It Down Classic: Creole Seasoning

Most folks simply grab a jar of Creole Seasoning in the supermarket these days but this recipe predates any packaged varieties. Rich with the spices and flavors that make Louisiana cooking the mouth-watering standard it is, homemade Creole Seasoning can be used to add flavor to meats, stews, soups, and even rice and casserole dishes. The best part is that our version is easy to make and preservative free.

¼ cup coarse salt
3 tablespoons garlic powder
2 tablespoons black pepper
2 tablespoons onion powder
2 tablespoons cayenne pepper
⅓ cup paprika
2 tablespoons dried parsley
2 tablespoons dried oregano
2 tablespoons dried thyme

Stir all ingredients until they are completely blended and store in an airtight container.

Denise Curry's Super Easy Spaghetti Sauce

Los Angeles, California

SERVES 4

"My mother used to make this sauce when I was a young girl. It is a little different from the conventional marinara type sauce. It's creamy and tomatoey, but it is still delicious," says Denise Curry. "I have made this sauce for years. It is simple and tasty. You can substitute ground turkey or chicken, add sliced Italian sausage, mushrooms, or any other ingredients that suit your tastes. The simpleness of this sauce makes it ideal for parties and pot lucks."

1 tablespoon olive oil
1 pound ground beef
1 cup onion, finely diced
1 cup bell pepper, finely diced
5 cloves garlic, finely chopped (reserve 2 cloves)
¼ cup chili powder
⅛ cup seasoning salt
⅛ cup Mrs. Dash or other salt-free seasoning
2 10.5-ounce cans cream of tomato soup
2 10.5-ounce cans cream of mushroom soup
1 box spaghetti, cooked according to package directions

Heat oil in large sauté pan and add onions and bell pepper. Sauté until onions are softened and add two cloves of garlic. Cook 1 minute more. Add the ground beef and stir well, cook until browned. Remove beef from pan with a slotted spoon and drain fat from pan.

Return beef mixture to the pan and add chili powder, seasoned salt, salt-free seasoning, and remaining garlic.

Add four cans of soup and stir well. Simmer on very low heat, stirring occasionally. Serve over cooked spaghetti.

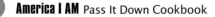

Antebellum Barbecue Sauce

Spartanburg, South Carolina

MAKES 1½ CUPS OF SAUCE

The narrative of Mr. Wesley Jones, who was born enslaved in South Carolina in 1840, is the source of this delicious barbecue sauce. In his narrative, edited by Elmer Turnage of the Works Projects Administration of the 1930s, he described his role as a pit-master at the many barbecues that served as social and business engagements for the planter class. Mr. Jones and many other men like him are the unsung creators of the Southern barbecue tradition. Historian Michael Twitty says that while some trace the origins of the word barbecue to a Carib term from the West Indies, barbacoa, other linguists point to words like babbake, which means to "grill, toast, or broil" from the Hausa language of northern Nigeria, as evidence that barbecue has equally strong roots in African and African American culture.

½ stick unsalted butter or margarine
1 large yellow or white onion, well chopped
2 cloves of garlic, minced
1 cup apple cider vinegar
½ cup water
1 tablespoon kosher salt
1 teaspoon black pepper
1 pod long red cayenne pepper or 1 teaspoon cayenne pepper flakes
1 teaspoon dried, rubbed sage
1 teaspoon dried basil leaves or 1 tablespoon minced fresh basil
½ teaspoon crushed coriander seed
¼ cup dark brown sugar or 4 tablespoons molasses (not blackstrap)

Melt butter in large saucepan over medium heat. Add onion and garlic, and sauté until translucent. Turn heat down slightly and add vinegar, water, any variation ingredients if using, and salt, black pepper, cayenne pepper, rubbed sage, basil, coriander, and sugar or molasses.

Cook gently for 30 minutes to an hour. Use as light mop sauce or glaze during the last 15–30 minutes over the pit of coals as well as a dip for cooked meat.

. . . .

Pass It Down variations: *Carolina Mustard Sauce: Add ½ cup or more of brown mustard to taste, and a bit more sugar to taste. Red Sauce: Add two cans of tomato paste or four very ripe red or purple heirloom tomatoes, such as Large Red, Cherokee Purple, Brandywine, or Amish Paste, cooked down for several hours on low heat into a comparable consistency; and two tablespoons of Worcestershire sauce.*

. . . .

Caramelly Chocolate Sauce

Olathe, Kansas

MAKES 1½ CUPS SAUCE

Renea Feagin uses this recipe most often to top her brownies, but it's great on ice cream too.

½ cup semisweet chocolate chips
1 can sweetened condensed milk
¼ teaspoon salt
2 egg yolks
¼ cup hot milk
1 teaspoon vanilla extract

In heavy saucepan over medium heat, stir together chocolate chips, sweetened condensed milk, and salt. Stir until chips melt and mixture is thick and bubbly, about 5 minutes.

Place the egg yolks in a small mixing bowl and whisk in hot milk, adding milk a little at a time, whisking the whole while so the eggs do not scramble. Add egg yolk mixture to melted chocolate mixture and whisk to combine.

Continue to cook until mixture is very thick and bubbly, about 1 minute. Set a fine mesh sieve over a medium-size mixing bowl and strain the chocolate mixture into the bowl, pressing with a rubber spatula to force the mixture through the sieve, if necessary. Discard any lumps.

Stir in vanilla and set mixture aside to cool, stirring occasionally.

CHAPTER

10

Beverages

Sweet Tea

Southern United States

MAKES 8 SERVINGS

Sweet tea, a highly sweetened, deeply steeped iced tea, is popular throughout the South all-year around. It's not just a summertime drink, as it is in the North and elsewhere, and folks will drink it by itself or with meals. The secret is boiling the sugar with the water and then adding the teabags to steep.

2 quarts (8 cups) cold water
1 cup sugar
4 Luziane tea bags, or other black tea bags

Place water in large pot and add sugar. Bring to a boil and stir so sugar totally dissolves.

Remove pot from heat and add tea bags. Cover and allow to steep 15 minutes.

Remove tea bags and allow tea to cool. Pour into a gallon pitcher or jar and add 2 more quarts of cold water. Store in refrigerator and enjoy anytime.

• •

Did You Know? *Sweet Tea is one of the South's oldest and most distinctive southern comforts. If you order Sweet Tea below the Mason-Dixon line, you would routinely be given a "long and strong" brewed, very highly sweetened iced beverage estimated to be about two times as sweet as your average soda.*

• •

"Sweet Tea is the house wine of the South."
— **Dolly Parton** in *Steel Magnolias*

• •

Pass It Down variation: *Watching your blood sugar? Try Stevia, an herb that naturally tastes sweeter than sugar and can be purchased as a powder or in liquid drops. To make sweet tea using Stevia, stir in the Stevia after removing the tea bags. You'll need 4 tablespoons of Stevia powder or 2½ teaspoons of liquid Stevia.*

• •

Watermelon Iced Tea

San Francisco, California

SERVES 8

Karen V. Clopton, a chief administrative law judge, says this recipe was passed down to her through her father Julius Clopton and one of his best friends, Frank Jimenez, who was from Mexico. "Almost every weekend our family and the Jimenez family got together and had dinner, alternating and merging the cooking honors. My father and Uncle Frank concocted this delicious refreshment from their two heritages: Uncle Frank's Mexican Agua Fresca with watermelon and my father's Southern sweet tea tradition and his love of watermelon," says Clopton. "Of course, now and then the adults would supplement their watermelon iced tea with a shot of tequila."

6 cups fresh brewed India black tea
6 cups fresh watermelon
1 cup of ice
2 cups distilled water

Make ahead: Fill ice cube trays with watermelon puree to freeze for a nice decorative and delicious addition to glasses when served.

Brew fresh pot of India black tea. Allow to cool to room temperature. Puree the fresh watermelon and cup of ice. Mix pureed watermelon and tea and pour into a 2-quart pitcher. Ratio: 2 parts watermelon to 1 part tea, depending on how sweet you prefer it.

Add 2 cups of distilled water.

Serve in tall frosted iced tea glasses over ice.

··· Tom Bullock ···

Source: Public Domain

Master bartender Tom Bullock was born just after the Civil War in Louisville, Kentucky. The exact trajectory to the height of his fame as master bartender of the St. Louis Country Club in St. Louis, Missouri is not clear, but what is certain is that his libations earned him praise from high society, politicians, and the common man alike. In 1917 he published a book called The Ideal Bartender, *the first cocktail recipe book by an African American. Among his most notable friends—and there were many—were August Busch of Anheuser-Busch, who had Mr. Bullock to thank for the creative uses he found for Bevo, the beer substitute the brewer created during Prohibition that kept the company in business and its workers employed.*

• •

"Who was ever known to drink just a part of one of Tom's? Tom, than whom there is no greater mixologist of any race, color or condition of servitude was taught the art of the julep by no less than Marse Lilburn G. McNair, the father of the julep . . . To believe that red-blooded man, and a true Colonel at that, ever stopped with just a part of one of those refreshments which have made St. Louis hospitality proverbial . . . is to strain credulity too far."

— **St. Louis Post Dispatch editorial from May 28, 1913, commenting on President Roosevelt's claim he merely had a small sip of one of Tom Bullock's famous mint juleps**

• •

Lemonade Apollinaris

MAKES 1 SERVING

Patrons enjoy cocktails at The Palm Bar Taven,
a Chicago "Negro Restaurant," in 1941.

Apollinaris is a sparkling mineral water that has been produced in Germany since 1852. It would have a been a key tool in the bartending kit of a master mixologist like Tom Bullock and he specifically calls for it in a number of recipes in The Ideal Bartender. *The bubbles make for a refreshing take on lemonade.*

⅔ cup crushed ice
1 tablespoon of bar (superfine) sugar
juice of 1 lemon
1 bottle of Apollinaris

Place the crushed ice in a tall glass and add the lemon and sugar.

Gently add enough Apollinaris to fill the glass. Stir gently with a long spoon. Serve.

Mint Julep—Kentucky Style

1 HEALTHY SERVING, OR 2 SMALL ONES

Easily Tom Bullock's most famous recipe and the one that caused no end of publicity trouble for an abstaining President Teddy Roosevelt, this mint julep recipe calls for a "half pony" of water, which equals to about ½ an ounce or ½ a shot. In Tom Bullock's day, as now, bartending terminology featured some creative terms like mickey, jigger, shots, jeroboams, and more.

1 sugar cube or 1 teaspoon of sugar
½ pony (½ shot) of water
2 jiggers (3 ounces) of bourbon
mint sprig

In a large mug or highball glass, mix sugar and water.

Fill the mug with crushed ice and add bourbon.

Garnish with mint sprig and serve.

Catawba Cobbler

MAKES 1 SERVING

Until Prohibition, the Hermann and Augusta areas just outside St. Louis were the country's most prolific wine-producing regions, growing grapes that were a hybrid of sweeter native North American varieties and traditional European wine grapes. Among these was Catawba, a red grape that was used to produce a sweet red wine as well as a pink blush variety. Tom Bullock no doubt made use of these local wines in many of his concoctions. The St. Louis area wine industry virtually disappeared after Prohibition but has enjoyed a resurgence in the last twenty-five years, with many high-end wineries taking up the old standards. Although Catawba may be difficult to find these days, you can experiment with any semi-sweet red wine or rosé.

½ cup crushed ice
1 teaspoon bar (superfine) sugar dissolved in ¼ cup water
1½ jiggers (1½ ounces) Catawba wine
1 orange slice
raspberries and pitted cherries for garnish

Place ice in a tall glass, add sugar mixture and wine, and stir well.

Add orange slice.

Garnish with raspberries and cherries.

Pass It Down Classic: Georgia White Peach Sangria

SERVES 12 TO 14

Down South, folks don't flock to beer or wine as a favorite refreshment. So if you really want to show the love and impress the host at a Southern family gathering or party, bring a flavored chilled drink like this Georgia White Peach Sangria.

3 ripe white peaches, halved, then sliced 1/3-inch thick
½ tangerine, halved, then sliced ¼-inch thick
1 lemon, sliced in 1/3-inch circles
2½ ounces of pineapple juice (for color)
¼ bottle choice of Riesling
1 bottle pinot grigio
½ ounce peach brandy
1½ ounces peach schnapps
1½ ounces Triple Sec
2 cups of 7UP

Mix all ingredients together in a large glass bowl. Allow to marinate in the ice box for 12 hours.

To serve: Add 5 ounces of mixture to glass (include 5–6 pieces of sliced peaches). Fill glass with ice and add a splash of soda water and a splash of 7UP.

Pomegranate Champagne Punch

SERVES 6

This contemporary update of Tom Bullock's champagne punch uses the sweet taste of pomegranate to add even more flavor. Experiment with a wide variety of syrups to create your very own signature punch.

juice of 1 lemon
4 ounces of superfine (bar) sugar
1 jigger of 1883 Pomegranate Syrup
1 quart bottle of Champagne
1 sliced orange
3 slices pineapple

In a large glass pitcher, mix the lemon juice, superfine sugar, pomegranate syrup, and Champagne and stir slowly.

Stir and drop in orange and pineapple slices.

Garnish with fruit and serve in champagne goblets.

• •

Did you know? *Pomegranate juice is an antioxidant superstar. It has the highest amount of antioxidants among all juices.*

• •

1883 De Philibert Routin produces extremely high quality natural syrups like the one for pomegranate used in this recipe—from watermelon and roasted hazelnut syrup to coconut and chai. These syrups contain no artificial flavoring or preservatives and are available online at Amazon.com.

Really Exciting Fruit Punch

SERVES 8 TO 10

"Nothing says summertime like family reunions. Every year my family and I get together to catch up, reminisce, and have an all around great time," says Jeniece Isley, founder of Get 'Em Girls. "This Really Exciting Fruit Punch is an absolute must. It's super easy, versatile, and you don't have to worry about the kids knocking over your beloved punch bowl. For an adult's-only version, substitute 750 ml or one bottle of Prosecco or sparkling white wine for 3 cups of sparkling water right before serving.

½ large seedless watermelon
1 12-ounce can frozen pink lemonade concentrate
1 6-ounce can frozen limeade concentrate
5 cups chilled sparkling water or seltzer
1 pint lime sherbet
1 lime, washed and thinly sliced

Trim just enough of the bottom of the watermelon half to create a flat base and stabilize it. Hollow out the watermelon by scooping out the flesh until only the pale green interior shows. Freeze the rind for at least 1 hour or until ready to make the punch.

To make the punch, puree 4 cups of watermelon pulp in batches in a blender until smooth. Transfer to a large bowl or pitcher. Stir the lemonade and limeade concentrate into the bowl with the puree until completely melted. Refrigerate until ready to serve; it can be made the night before.

When ready to serve, pour the sparkling water or seltzer into the punch mixture and gently stir to combine. Pour the punch into the watermelon shell and float small scoops of the sherbet on top of the punch. Garnish with the lime slices and serve immediately.

Pass It Down Classic Homemade Eggnog

SERVES 8 TO 10

This special holiday treat is simple to make and can be stored in the icebox for 3–4 days. The Jamaican rum gives the beverage a little kick, but can be left out so the kids can enjoy it too.

8 egg yolks
1 cup sugar
4 cups milk
2 cinnamon sticks
3 whole cloves
2 cups heavy cream
2 teaspoons vanilla extract
3 teaspoons freshly grated nutmeg
3 tablespoons Jamaican rum or to taste

In a large bowl, beat egg yokes by hand thoroughly. Then slowly stream in the sugar and whisk until fluffy. Add the milk, cinnamon, and cloves in a heavy-bottomed pot. Slowly heat mixture on medium heat until hot, but not boiling.

Temper the eggs by slowly adding half of the hot milk mixture into the eggs while whisking constantly. Pour the mixture back into the saucepan.

Cook on medium heat, stirring repeatedly with a wooden spoon until the mixture begins to thicken and coats the back of the spoon. Do not allow the mixture to boil or it will curdle. However, if the mixture does curdle, you may be able to save it by running it through a blender.

Remove from heat and stir in the cream. Strain the mixture using a strainer to remove the cloves. Let cool for one hour.

Mix in the vanilla extract, nutmeg, and Jamaican rum. Serve cold or warm.

Generation Next:

Cooking with Kids and Young Chefs

··· Jumping into Taste ···

Exploring the Pleasure of Cooking with Kids

BY CHEF SCOTT ALVES BARTON

Since his first days as pot washer to the chefs at a country club when he was just 14 and a half years old, Scott Alves Barton has continually worked as a baker, executive chef, culinary consultant, and teacher to children and adults. He was honored in the first crop of Ebony magazine's top African American and African chefs. He has been invited to cook at the James Beard House and has been featured on national television. Currently, Chef Barton is completing research fellowships in the culinary history of Bahia, Brazil and Macao, China, as well as his doctoral work in food studies at New York University in Manhattan.

My road to becoming an executive chef began somewhere just around the middle of my third year. My mother, Sylvia, an educator and nutritionist who had once dreamed of becoming a great chef, expanded our horizons for play and taste by making our family kitchen a structured "play" center.

We were given the simplest tasks at first—counting out eggs and learning to measure with special spoons and cups. We later learned to make our favorite dishes, snacks, and sweets. Not long after, we began taking turns preparing part or all of the family dinner with her. In this way, she passed on her love of food and sense of culinary adventure to us, as she allowed us to explore a variety of foods, flavors, textures, aromas, cultures, and rituals used in preparing, serving, and eating our meals.

As we grew, my brother Craig and I were taught how to make whatever dish was our favorite. This allowed us a certain independence in the kitchen. By junior high school our chores included making some part or all of the family meal on a rotating basis. This helped my folks out, since they both worked all day. When Mom came home we often finished up the hard bits of the meal, and after dinner and homework we planned our next culinary adventure.

We nurture our children and check their progress in many ways, observing their capabilities with gross and fine motor skills, alphabets, and numbers. These simple activities and tests can serve as a clue to their potential and provide tools they'll use throughout life.

Unfortunately, we often wait until they're teenagers to think about educating their sense of taste, a valuable tool that will guide them throughout their lives. Whether we use taste to determine freshness and protect us from tainted foods as primitive man did, or for sensory pleasure and better nutrition, we need to stimulate our palates to foster good eating habits and ensure a love of diverse foods. This special section can be a jumping off point for both you and your children to enter a new world.

When cooking with your kids, I always stress good hygiene in all culinary activities. It is especially important that adults supervise when fire and sharp objects are used. Beyond the caution, remember that with guidance and supervision, many tasks can become adventures. With a zip-lock bag, a plastic disposable knife, and a few tools, young chefs can build their skills. The kitchen can be a laboratory to explore various subjects—mathematics, history, science, economics, anthropology, etc.

If we embrace the opportunities offered in our kitchens, a thousand worlds, flavors, and people will grace our dinners.

Mango Lassie

Chef Barton notes that in India, this traditional beverage is both cooling and nutritious. Curiously, it usually has enough salt to give it a bite, yet it still fights dehydration that can occur in hot, subtropical countries wherever mangoes are plentiful. In America you can decide how you want to season it. Once you've mastered mango lassies, experiment with other fruits, such as bananas, pears, or combinations of various seasonal fruits.

FOR EACH CHILD

1 ripe mango or frozen mango purée
4 ounces plain yogurt
¼ cup cold milk or water
pinch brown sugar, if desired
freshly squeezed juice of ½ lime

TOOLS

covered quart container
long spoon for stirring
drinking cup
whisk, if needed

If desired, you can substitute soy milk for yogurt and add 2 tablespoons of soft tofu to turn this into a protein shake.

Peel mango, discard skin. Cut away the big seed by slicing directly through the fruit from tip to tip, around the edge of the seed. (You could try to sprout it in water like an avocado for a science project.) Cut the largest pieces into 1–2-inch pieces and purée them in a blender. This should give you about 1 cup of puréed mangoes.

Using a spatula, scrape the purée into a quart container with a tight-fitting lid. Or, if using store-bought purée, simply place in the pint container with tight-fitting lid.

Place the yogurt, water, sugar, and lime juice into the container. Now it's time for your young chef partner to step in. Carefully secure the cover tightly on your container. Holding the container firmly with two hands, shake and blend, and let your young chef GO! Alternatively, you can let your young chef whisk the ingredients together by hand.

Taste to adjust for more sugar or lime juice as needed.

Old-Fashioned Buttermilk Hotcakes

Have children smell and taste buttermilk, nutmeg, and cornmeal for texture and flavor.

FOR EACH CHILD

1 egg
¾ cup buttermilk
1 tablespoon butter, melted
½ cup all-purpose flour
¼ cup stone-ground cornmeal
1 teaspoon baking powder
pinch salt
pinch nutmeg
½ pint strawberries, hulled and cut into quarters for garnish
yogurt as garnish (optional)
maple syrup
wheat germ as garnish (optional)

TOOLS

2 bowls, wooden spoon, and spatula
griddle or cast iron skillet
pancake spatula

Have each ingredient in a separate container for each child.

In one bowl, combine egg, buttermilk, and butter. Stir to blend. Stir together the flour, cornmeal, baking powder, salt, and nutmeg. Mix into egg mixture and stir until just combined. If batter is a bit lumpy, that's a good thing. Over-mixed is a bad thing.

Heat griddle and lightly grease. Drop batter by spoonfuls onto griddle. Cook over medium heat and watch for bubbles to form on the top surface.

Let the cakes brown on one side and flip over. Do not flip twice. Serve warm, with syrup, yogurt, wheat germ, and fresh fruit.

Fragrant Jerk Chicken

Caribbean Style BBQ Chicken is wonderfully spicy—but not too spicy. This recipe provides a great opportunity to engage our noses and tongues, smelling and tasting each herb or spice as we add it to our marinade. Talk about where these plants come from, underground, up in trees, etc.

FOR EACH CHILD

2 scallions, coarsely chopped with root removed

4 tablespoons olive oil

1 boneless skinless chicken breast, cut in half or in strips

1 clove garlic, finely minced

3 tablespoons freshly squeezed orange juice

3 tablespoons freshly squeezed lime juice

salt and freshly ground pepper, to taste

1 tablespoon fresh ginger root, finely minced

1–2 slices finger pepper, optional (can use as a smell sample!)

1 tablespoon soy sauce

¼ teaspoon ground allspice

½ teaspoon ground cinnamon

¼ teaspoon ground cloves

In a small blender, purée scallions and olive oil. Set aside in a container.

Place chicken in zip-top bag. Add the scallions and olive oil mixture. Next, add the rest of the ingredients to your bag and identify by taste, smell, and color. Seal the bag and allow the children to moosh, squoosh, and squeeze the bag to mix the spice mixture into the chicken. You can allow the chicken to marinate for up to 24 hours.

When ready to cook, heat a grill, oven (350° F), or broiler, and place chicken pieces on a grill pan or in a baking dish. Cook completely, turning once, about 20 minutes.

Serve warm or at room temperature.

Pass It Down trick: *Tuck into the kids' lunch bags with small whole-wheat pita breads for a protein-rich and yummy lunch.*

Moroccan Carrots

Chef Barton Kid-Friendly Recipe

Fragrant, lightly sweet, and aromatic—a tasty and simple addition to any dinner.

FOR EACH CHILD

1 tablespoon olive oil
½ tablespoon light brown sugar
⅓ teaspoon ground cinnamon
¼ teaspoon ground cumin
dash cayenne pepper, or to taste
1½ cups carrots (about ½ pound), cut into slices or strips
⅓ cup orange juice
2½ tablespoons dried currants, soaked in hot water
black pepper, freshly ground
parsley or mint, chopped, for garnish

Heat olive oil in large saucepan over moderate heat. Reduce heat to low. Add sugar, cinnamon, cumin, cayenne pepper, and carrots. Stir for a few minutes.

Add orange juice and currants with some of their soaking liquid. Bring mixture to a boil then quickly reduce heat and simmer, covered, until carrots are tender, about 20 minutes.

Add pepper and adjust the seasoning to taste. Sprinkle with chopped parsley or mint. Makes 4 half-cup servings.

Chewy Granola & Dried Fruit Bars

This homemade granola bar contains seeds that are rich in brain-building omega fatty acids. Dried fruit, tang, and sweetness—great for a midmorning snack!

FOR EACH CHILD

¼ cup vegetable oil
2 cups old-fashioned rolled oats
¼ teaspoon salt
½ teaspoon cinnamon
½ cup honey or sorghum
⅓ cup light brown sugar
1 cup sunflower seeds
1 cup dried fruit (apricots, dates, raisins), coarsely chopped
½ cup nuts, chopped (optional)
¼ cup sesame seeds
1 tablespoon flax seeds

TOOLS

small saucepan
wooden spoon
1 lb. baking dish
rubber spatula

Preheat oven to 350° F. In a small bowl, combine oats, salt, cinnamon, and oil. Stir to blend. Spread oats on baking sheet and bake for 10 minutes until golden. Cool and reserve.

In a small saucepan, add honey or sorghum and sugar. Stir and bring to a boil. Simmer five minutes. Remove from heat. Let cool slightly.

Stir in sunflower seeds, dried fruit, chopped nuts (if using), sesame seeds, and flax seeds.

Pour and scrape oat mixture into lightly oiled baking dish, spreading batter so it's evenly distributed in the pan. Bake 15 minutes or until golden brown.

Let cool. Cut into squares.

Mac and Please

Las Vegas, Nevada

SERVES 6

Source: Meghan Poorst

Stacy Henderson with husband Chef Jeff and kids

Stacy Henderson, the wife of Chef Jeff, is a fabulous cook in her own right. As the mother of four vegan children, she has to be creative in the kitchen and come up with innovative meals that are nutritious using non-animal ingredients. "This dish is my take on the classic mac and cheese," she says. "After tweaking this recipe numerous times, I finally mastered a tasty side dish that is sure to please."

FOR EACH CHILD

1 teaspoon olive oil

1 pinch of salt

1 16-ounce package wheat elbow macaroni (or pasta of your choice)

4 cups non-dairy shredded Daiya cheddar cheese

3 tablespoons non-dairy butter, softened (I prefer Earth Balance)

sea salt and black pepper to taste

3 tablespoons organic non-bleached flour

3 cups unsweetened rice or soy milk

1 cup of panko bread crumbs

1 pinch smoked paprika

TOOLS

large pot

large bowl

baking dish

Preheat oven to 350° F.

Bring a large pot of water to a boil. Add the olive oil and a pinch of salt. Add the pasta and cook for 6–8 minutes, until al dente. Drain pasta and pour into a large bowl. Mix 3 cups of cheese into the pasta and set aside.

In a small pot, melt the butter. Add salt and pepper, then slowly whisk in flour until fully incorporated. Stir in the milk. Bring mixture to boil, then continue to stir until mixture slightly thickens. (Sauce should not have the appearance of a paste.)

Pour the non-dairy milk mixture into the pasta and mix well. Transfer to a greased baking dish. Note: If you pack the pasta in a small baking dish, it will set properly. Top with the remaining cheese and cover pasta with a generous layer of panko bread crumbs.

Sprinkle lightly with paprika. Bake uncovered in the oven for 30 minutes or until the cheese is bubbling and the top is lightly browned.

Whipped Sweet Potatoes

Las Vegas, Nevada

SERVES 6

This perfect kid-friendly recipe was inspired by Jeff Henderson's aunt Barbara Kendrick. "Aunt Barbara is an excellent home cook and makes the most delightful whipped sweet potatoes I have ever tasted," Stacy Henderson says. "This is my remake of her popular side dish. My kids give it two thumbs up and can make it all by themselves."

FOR EACH CHILD

3 large sweet potatoes, scrubbed
4 tablespoons non-dairy butter, softened (I prefer Earth Balance)
2 tablespoons organic brown sugar (or blue agave nectar syrup)
½ teaspoon ground cinnamon
1 pinch freshly grated nutmeg
¼ teaspoon vanilla extract

TOOLS

roasting pan
plastic fork
plastic spoon
large bowl

Preheat the oven to 400° F. Place 3 large sweet potatoes on a roasting pan. Pierce each one 2 or 3 times with a fork. Bake for 1–1½ hours or until tender. Scoop out sweet potato flesh into a large bowl. Add non-dairy butter, organic brown sugar, cinnamon, nutmeg, and vanilla. Whip the potatoes until smooth and fluffy. Serve immediately.

···Sacred Table, Sacred Feast···

BY DESMONETTE HAZLY

Source: Maryum Ali

Desmonette Hazly discovered the power of using food for social change while pursuing her master's degree in social work. She received her culinary arts diploma at a local cooking school in Los Angeles and attended the Cordon Bleu in London and Paris while she completed her Ph.D. in International Politics and Policy. She is the chair of the International Services Ambassador program for the American Red Cross and consults with non-profits and government agencies in Los Angeles and developing countries to create programs to stimulate community and economic growth in small cities and improve the quality of life for the disadvantaged.

I arrive to teach my cooking class to a setting perfectly arranged for preparing a feast. White tablecloths, colorful cutting boards, and shiny clean utensils to prepare the meal are respectfully placed at each setting. The table is filled with fresh fruits and vegetables, and anything else nutritious my students will need to prepare a beautiful three-course gourmet meal. They are in an environment that shows them respect and nurtures peaceful interaction. And they return their respect by opening themselves to a new experience and respecting everyone around them. They are young and old. Black and brown. Gang member, kindergartener, and grandmother. Everyone knows that they are in a safe and sacred space, and they are each the guest of honor.

This is no regular culinary school or high-end cooking class. It is a culinary arts workshop that the city of Los Angeles, where I live, has asked me to develop using my culinary arts skills from my training as a professional chef. The goal is to use communal preparation of food and the ritual of dining together as a means to bring communities together that are struggling with gang violence and racial tensions, as part of the Los Angeles Summer Night Lights (SNL) program.

Mayor Villaraigosa launched the SNL program in 2008 to combat gang violence during summer months. This program engages all members of the community by providing job opportunities, free food, athletic leagues, cultural arts programming, and other positive activities for families from 7 P.M. to midnight—the peak hours of gang violence—in selected locations that are in high crime areas. In 2010, I joined the program, providing my culinary arts workshops at all of the 24 citywide SNL locations.

Each of these classes reminds me that food is a universal language that transcends all barriers and boundaries. It communicates the most simple and complex ideas and concepts while engaging the senses and emotions. What we eat and how we share our meals with each other defines our identity, tells our histories, and expresses our present—and our hopes and dreams of the future—as individuals and as a community. This is the power of food and the ritual of breaking bread together.

As a scholar, educator, and community advocate, I have always struggled to find the best means to reach all people and improve the communities I serve. Here in Los Angeles, communities segregate themselves and cross-cultural communication is a challenge. For me to work with multiethnic communities that face various issues, I had to develop a strategy that everyone could understand and embrace. Cooking has proven a powerful and universally effective tool for social change.

Culinary arts allows me to collaborate with a global community to creatively address many socio-economic challenges. Teaching reading and writing to adults who had given up on becoming literate, promoting self-reliance and independence for women who found themselves living on Skid Row, and encouraging self-worth and social responsibility for at-risk youth who are considering gang membership, have been some of the ways I have used culinary arts to improve the community.

The participants come to the classes excited but skeptical that they are about to create something special, let alone something special enough that others will admire. In a crisp pressed chef uniform, I go over the menu and the ingredients for the evening as nervous, uncertain smirks turn into big smiles and energetic chatter. At this point everyone is eager to dive into making their gourmet meal.

Conversation ensues effortlessly among strangers from different backgrounds, and together they embark on a culinary adventure that allows them to create freely. Laughter, eye contact, and helpful hints flow abundantly among the newly formed culinary family. They are fully engaged and empowered by the act of culinary communion. They show each other love and praise with no shame. There is nothing more powerful than surprising yourself with a new skill and sharing that skill with people who are just as excited as you are.

They admire each other's edible artistic interpretations and happily offer compliments to people they do not know. They eagerly rush to show family, friends, and anyone who happens to be passing by what they have created and proudly exclaim, "I Made This!"

By the time all meals are made and people are indulging in their creations, no one seems to notice the bonds that have been forged. Strangers continue their conversations as they walk outside together, enjoying an interaction and fellowship with people they usually would not talk to in their own community. There are no enemies here—only a sacred table with a sacred feast prepared by a healing, sacred community.

GENERATION NEXT CHEFS

Chef Jeff with young chefs (left to right) Mical Terry, Nickalas Reid, Tara Gardner, and Donnell Jones-Craven, students at The International Culinary School at The Art Institute of Atlanta.

"Each one teach one" has been one of the most effective ways to school the next generation on how to get things done. In the past, cooking in the kitchen alongside relatives, friends, and neighbors established a permanent kinship and a cultural legacy. It was how each generation learned to develop their cooking chops. Today, in our fast-food nation, many young chefs of color are being introduced to their food heritage at culinary schools and are encouraged to reclaim those traditions. By exploring the African American food universe, young chefs learn to cook, taste, and create new worlds.

When generations cook alongside one another they are infused with an unbreakable bond. This is why I am committed to reaching back to give opportunities to the next generation of chefs, caterers, bakers, and home cooks—to continue the legacy of passing it down. In the section that follows, we salute this next generation of culinary artists for their passion, creativity, and commitment to our influential food history.

Mama and Mical's Pickled Eggs

Riverside, California

SERVES 3 TO 6

Source: M. Elizabeth Wilson

Mical Terry is a student at The International Culinary School at the Art Institute of Atlanta and a recipient of the school's Chef Jeff Henderson Scholarship. Terry says her passion for food was instilled by her mother, who was raised in the West but remained a lover of down home soul. In Terry's family there are many recipes, but she is committed to recreating family favorites with her own special signature added to the traditional flavors that mean so much.

1 18-ounce can of beets
16 ounces apple cider vinegar
1 teaspoon salt
2 jalapeno peppers
1 dozen eggs
1 32-ounce jar with seal

Place the beets, apple cider vinegar, teaspoon of salt, and jalapenos in a medium-size sauce pan. Let mixture come to a simmer in order to marry the flavors. While waiting for cider mixture to simmer, boil and peel the eggs.

Once mixture begins to simmer, place peeled eggs in a 32-ounce jar and then pour the cider mixture over eggs. Place a piece of aluminum foil over the opening of the jar. Seal jar off and place in a room-temperature location for one week.

When seal is broken, you can eat and enjoy. The eggs should be purple all the way through to the yolk, and will have a bit of spice because of the jalapenos.

Sweet Water Creek Hush Puppies

Atlanta, Georgia

SERVES 4

Generation Next Chef

Source: Joel Rickerson

Joel Rickerson is a third-generation chef and restaurateur from Atlanta, Georgia. His father, Chef Joe Rickerson, has more than 30 years of experience in fine dining and personal services for some of America's top restaurants and celebrities. Today, they co-own SPACE Atlanta Restaurant and Lounge, located in the historic West End area of Atlanta. Rickerson says Sweet Water Creek Hush Puppies were first created during slavery, and they often accompanied fried mullet because that was the only type of fish readily available to African Americans.

1 cup self-rising cornmeal
½ tablespoon black pepper
½ teaspoon salt
2 teaspoons chopped scallions
1 egg
4 teaspoons vegetable oil
½ cup milk

Mix all ingredients well. Let sit in the refrigerator for 15 minutes. Heat skillet with oil to 350° F. Scoop mixture up with a small ice cream scooper or tablespoon and place in the skillet. Once placed in oil, mixture will form into balls. Let cook for 8–10 minutes, then let cool for 2–3 minutes. Serve with tartar sauce.

Memphis Style BBQ Beef Tenderloin Sliders

Memphis, Tennessee

SERVES 10

Source: Luvena Campbell

Luvena Campbell developed a love for cooking in her early 20s when she began working in a local restaurant as a server. Her passion for the culinary arts led her to pursue a bachelor's degree in food service management from Johnson & Wales University. Campbell now works as a sous chef for Compass Group America, one of the nation's largest food service companies. In the near future, she wants to take on the role of executive chef. Campbell likes this beef tenderloin recipe because it offers servings in small portions but still leaves people full and happy.

BEEF TENDERLOINS

¼ cup olive oil
1 teaspoon black pepper
1 teaspoon salt
1 teaspoon fresh thyme
1 teaspoon garlic power
5 pounds raw beef tenderloin
1 12-count package of Hawaiian Sweet Rolls or other small bread rolls

Combine seasonings. Dredge tenderloin evenly with seasoning. Cover and refrigerate 6 hours or overnight, if possible.

On clean grill, sear all sides and ends. Place tenderloins in roasting pan.

Preheat oven to 425° F.

Place tenderloins in oven and roast until desired temperature is reached.

Slice tenderloin in 2–3 ounce portions. Hold warm until assembly .

MEMPHIS BARBEQUE SAUCE

1 tablespoon butter
¼ cup onion, finely chopped
1½ cups ketchup
¼ cup chili sauce
4 tablespoons brown sugar
4 tablespoons molasses
2 tablespoons ground yellow mustard
1 tablespoon fresh lemon juice
1 tablespoon Worcestershire sauce
1 tablespoon liquid hickory smoke
1 tablespoon red pepper flakes
½ teaspoon garlic powder
salt and pepper to taste

In a saucepan, slowly sauté onions in butter until soft and translucent. Add remaining ingredients. Simmer for about 20 minutes. Taste and adjust seasonings.

Place tenderloin pieces on warm slider bread. Add 1 tablespoon of barbeque sauce.

Thyme Sweet Potato Fries

Memphis, Tennessee

SERVES 10

"This recipe offers a delicious alternative to regular French fries, and your waist line won't suffer because they're baked instead of fried," says Luvena Campbell.

10 sweet potatoes cut to look large French fries
½ cup water
2 tablespoons olive oil
½ cup thyme
salt and pepper to taste

Preheat oven 400°F.

Place the cut sweet potatoes in a microwave-safe dish with the water. Cook in microwave for about 8 minutes. Drain liquid and toss with oil and seasonings.

Arrange fries on baking sheet in single layer.

Bake for 30 minutes, turning once, or until fries are crispy on the outside.

Donte' Johnson's Blackened Salmon

Las Vegas, Nevada

SERVES 4 TO 6

Source: Donté Johnson

Donte' Johnson, an up-and-coming pastry chef in Las Vegas, graduated from Le Cordon Bleu of Las Vegas in 2006. He now owns Pastries by Donte'. Though his passion may be decorating whimsical wedding cakes, he also knows a thing or two about savory cooking. His inspiration for this Creole classic came from him wanting to do something different for Sunday dinner. "Adding the garlic and ginger last to the sauce gives the fish a new in-depth flavor combination," he says.

4–6 salmon fillets, skin off and rinsed
1 cup butter
½ cup fresh-squeezed lemon juice
2 tablespoons Cajun, Creole, or blackening spice mix
2 tablespoons chopped fresh garlic
2 tablespoons chopped fresh ginger

Rinse fillets and pat dry. Set aside.

Melt butter in microwave-safe bowl. Once melted, mix in lemon juice and set aside until butter mixture has become warm to the touch.

Dip fillets in butter mixture. Once the fillets have been coated, sprinkle spice mix onto both sides of the fish and then gently pat it onto the fish a bit more.

Heat cast iron pan or a heavy frying pan until it beings to smoke, about 6–8 minutes. Place the fillets in the hot skillet, cooking 2–3 minutes on each side. Repeat as needed for remaining fillets.

Once all fillets have been cooked, set aside in the oven to keep warm. Wipe skillet clean and return to stove top. On medium heat, add remaining butter mixture, garlic, and ginger to pan to make the sauce. Continuously stir sauce until the garlic and ginger become aromatic, about 2–3 minutes.

Drizzle sauce over fillet with a side of rice and sautéed vegetables.

Saporous Strawberry Cheesecake

Generation Next Chef

Las Vegas, Nevada

SERVES 12

Donte' Johnson says it's the sauce that distinguishes his Saporous (meaning delicious) Strawberry Cheesecake from others. "Using either fresh or frozen strawberries, the sauce adds a freshness to this dessert, leaving you and your loved ones completely satisfied," he says.

THE CRUST

2 cups finely crushed vanilla wafers
¼ cup granulated white sugar
½ cup unsalted butter, melted

THE FILLING

4 8-ounce packages of cream cheese, room temperature
1 cup granulated white sugar
3 tablespoons all-purpose flour
5 large eggs, room temperature
1/3 cup whole milk, room temperature
1 teaspoon lemon extract
1 teaspoon pure vanilla extract

THE STRAWBERRY SAUCE

1 pint fresh strawberries, cleaned, or 16 ounces thawed frozen strawberries
¼ cup of sugar
1 teaspoon pure vanilla extract

Preheat oven to 350° F with rack in center of the oven.

THE CRUST

In a medium-size bowl, combine the vanilla wafer crumbs, sugar, and melted butter. Spray a 9-inch springform pan with non-stick vegetable spray. Press the crumbs evenly over the bottom of the springform pan. Bake in the oven at 350° F for 10 minutes. Once baked, remove from oven to cool.

THE FILLING

In the bowl of your electric mixer, place the cream cheese, sugar, and flour. Beat on medium speed until smooth, scraping down the bowl as needed. One at a time, add the eggs, beating well. Scrape down the sides of the bowl. Add the whole milk, vanilla extract, and lemon extract. Beat until incorporated. Do not over mix. Retrieve crust and pour in the filling. Bake for 1 hour at 350° F, or until firm and only the center of the cheesecake looks a little wet. Remove from oven and carefully run a knife or spatula around the inside edge of pan to loosen the cheesecake and help prevent cracking.

THE STRAWBERRY SAUCE

Using a blender, combine the fresh or thawed strawberries, sugar, and vanilla extract. Begin on a low setting and increase speed to medium. Once completely smooth, turn blender off. Pour strawberry sauce on top of cooled cheesecake. Serve with whipped cream.

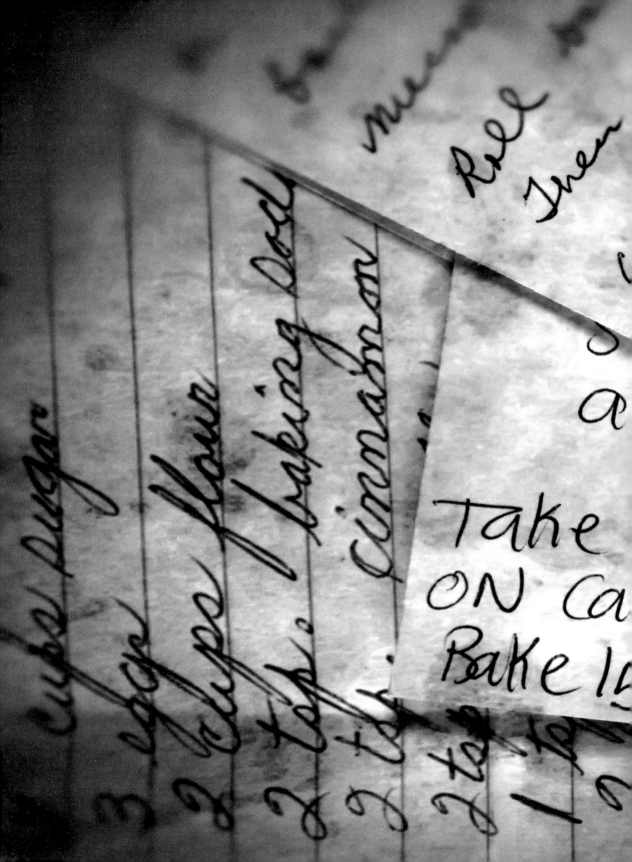

12

Your Pass It Down Recipes

· · · It's Your Turn to Pass It Down · · ·

BY JONELL NASH

Jonell Nash is the former Essence magazine food editor. Her cookbooks have included Low-Fat Soul *and* Essence Brings You Great Cooking. *Ms. Nash served as one of the judges for the* America I AM Pass It Down Cookbook Recipe Contest.

In the early days of our history in America, a satisfying meal was one of the few joys. Today, we often take for granted the wonder and enchantment of mouth-watering soul food as we sit down to Sunday dinner. Our ancestors pieced together amazing meals in their makeshift pantries with produce from their gardens along with seafood and game caught in local waters and nearby woods. Greens, okra, sweet peppers, corn, lima beans, shrimp, crawfish, catfish, possum, and rabbit became the makings of flavorful dishes that held together body, mind, and spirit.

Then, as now, our food was integral to the stories of our lives—weddings, christenings, rites of passage, anniversaries, and wakes. We asked our contributors to keep in mind the food imprint history of their recipe contributions. Now we extend that challenge to you.

By inviting family members and friends to share their favorite recipes—ingredient by ingredient and memory by memory—we not only honor the inheritance gifted to us by the original culinary architects of the food we treasure, we create a priceless oral and written keepsake of shared memories for generations to come.

Pass It Down!

Recipe Name:

SERVINGS:

RECIPE HISTORY:

_____

_____

_____

_____

INGREDIENTS:

_____   _____

_____   _____

_____   _____

_____   _____

_____   _____

_____   _____

_____   _____

_____   _____

_____   _____

INSTRUCTIONS:

_____

_____

_____

_____

_____

_____

_____

_____

_____

_____

Recipe Name:

SERVINGS:

RECIPE HISTORY:

_____

_____

_____

_____

_____

INGREDIENTS:

_____   _____

_____   _____

_____   _____

_____   _____

_____   _____

_____   _____

_____   _____

_____   _____

_____   _____

_____   _____

_____   _____

INSTRUCTIONS:

_____

_____

_____

_____

_____

_____

_____

_____

_____

_____

_____

_____

Recipe Name:

SERVINGS:

RECIPE HISTORY:

_____
_____
_____
_____

INGREDIENTS:

_____   _____
_____   _____
_____   _____
_____   _____
_____   _____
_____   _____
_____   _____
_____   _____
_____   _____
_____   _____

INSTRUCTIONS:

_____
_____
_____
_____
_____
_____
_____
_____
_____
_____

Recipe Name:

SERVINGS:

RECIPE HISTORY:

_____

_____

_____

_____

INGREDIENTS:

_____   _____

_____   _____

_____   _____

_____   _____

_____   _____

_____   _____

_____   _____

_____   _____

_____   _____

_____   _____

INSTRUCTIONS:

_____

_____

_____

_____

_____

_____

_____

_____

_____

_____

_____

_____

Recipe Name:

SERVINGS:

RECIPE HISTORY:

_____

_____

_____

_____

_____

INGREDIENTS:

_____   _____

_____   _____

_____   _____

_____   _____

_____   _____

_____   _____

_____   _____

_____   _____

_____   _____

_____   _____

INSTRUCTIONS:

_____

_____

_____

_____

_____

_____

_____

_____

_____

_____

Recipe Name:

SERVINGS:

RECIPE HISTORY:

_____

_____

_____

_____

INGREDIENTS:

_____   _____

_____   _____

_____   _____

_____   _____

_____   _____

_____   _____

_____   _____

_____   _____

INSTRUCTIONS:

_____

_____

_____

_____

_____

_____

_____

_____

_____

_____

_____

Recipe Name:

SERVINGS:

RECIPE HISTORY:

_____
_____
_____
_____

INGREDIENTS:

_____ _____
_____ _____
_____ _____
_____ _____
_____ _____
_____ _____
_____ _____
_____ _____
_____ _____
_____ _____

INSTRUCTIONS:

_____
_____
_____
_____
_____
_____
_____
_____
_____
_____

Recipe Name:

SERVINGS:

RECIPE HISTORY:

_____
_____
_____
_____

INGREDIENTS:

_____   _____
_____   _____
_____   _____
_____   _____
_____   _____
_____   _____
_____   _____
_____   _____
_____   _____
_____   _____
_____   _____

INSTRUCTIONS:

_____
_____
_____
_____
_____
_____
_____
_____
_____
_____

Recipe Name:

SERVINGS:

RECIPE HISTORY:

_____

_____

_____

_____

INGREDIENTS:

_____   _____

_____   _____

_____   _____

_____   _____

_____   _____

_____   _____

_____   _____

_____   _____

_____   _____

INSTRUCTIONS:

_____

_____

_____

_____

_____

_____

_____

_____

_____

_____

Recipe Name:

SERVINGS:

RECIPE HISTORY:

_____
_____
_____
_____

INGREDIENTS:

_____   _____
_____   _____
_____   _____
_____   _____
_____   _____
_____   _____
_____   _____
_____   _____
_____   _____
_____   _____

INSTRUCTIONS:

_____
_____
_____
_____
_____
_____
_____
_____
_____
_____
_____

Recipe Name:

SERVINGS:

RECIPE HISTORY:

_____

_____

_____

_____

INGREDIENTS:

_____   _____

_____   _____

_____   _____

_____   _____

_____   _____

_____   _____

_____   _____

_____   _____

_____   _____

_____   _____

INSTRUCTIONS:

_____

_____

_____

_____

_____

_____

_____

_____

_____

_____

Recipe Name:

SERVINGS:

RECIPE HISTORY:

_____
_____
_____
_____

INGREDIENTS:

_____ _____
_____ _____
_____ _____
_____ _____
_____ _____
_____ _____
_____ _____
_____ _____
_____ _____
_____ _____

INSTRUCTIONS:

_____
_____
_____
_____
_____
_____
_____
_____
_____
_____

Acknowledgments

This work could never have been made possible without the *pass it down* recipes and inspiring stories that African American home cooks and accomplished chefs from throughout the U.S. contributed to this heritage cookbook. *Thank you! Thank you! Thank you!*

Our deep gratitude goes to our ancestors and elders who dared to document African American food history through the rich oral and experiential tradition of each-one-teach-one. In the modern era, we thank everyone who has expanded our understanding and respect for African American foodways through cookbooks, writings, and food products.

Thanks to Tavis Smiley for the America I AM vision and to Denise Pines for tapping me with the honor of shepherding this special project into the world.

My infinite gratitude goes to my co-editor, Ramin Ganeshram, whose creativity, journalistic skill, passion, and knowledge of African Americans' contributions to the evolution of cuisine in America has been priceless.

The SmileyBooks editorial team truly guided us and kept this project alive and moving. Special thanks to the editor behind the editors, SmileyBooks' president Cheryl Woodruff. Whether serving as my sous chef on the road as we solicited recipes or working elbow to elbow with her staff behind the scenes, Cheryl never left the kitchen no matter how hot it got. Special kudos to SmileyBooks' editorial staffers Chaz Kyser and Kirsten Melvey for their commitment, dedication, and follow-through.

A very special shout out to goes to our brilliant designer Charles McStravick of Hay House. Charles not only captured our vision, he translated the warmth and love in our hearts on every page.

As always, thank you to my wife Stacy, whose patience, commitment to our family and my work as a chef, is evident in all that I have accomplished over the past decade.

To my children and all the young folks, we documented our experience for you to grow, benefit, and *"pass it down"* to future generations. We look forward to the special contributions that you alone are destined to make to the world.

— **Jeff Henderson,**
NOVEMBER 2010

In all my years as a food writer working on projects large and small, I have never experienced such an outpouring of love and excitement for a project as I have with this book. The energy and joyful sharing of family recipes and stories has been a wonder to behold. You'll see some notable names in this book, but you'll mostly see real folks who have brought us into their kitchens and made us part of their families. To each one of them we say, "Thank you!"

What you won't be able to see is the monumental behind-the-scenes efforts of folks who joined in supporting this project because they believed wholeheartedly in its value. Each and every one of them has lent effort, time, contacts, and most of all, mad-crazy cheerleading as we put this book together. Michele Washington deserves big props for taking up the role of girl-reporter and painstakingly taking down folks' recipes, while offering a few of her own. Noted Chef Scott Alves Barton's special kids' recipes truly make this book have something for everyone.

Our essayists, Adrian Miller, Dr. Donna Daniels, Dr. Desmonette Hazly, The Duo Dishes and, again, the intrepid Ms. Michele Washington, have added rich color and depth to the brilliantly complex tapestry that is the story of African American food. Michael Twitty, respected African foodways historian, was kind enough to share the story of his conversion to Judaism and how that brought him even closer to his soul food heritage. Thanks to Guy-Oreido Weston for sharing the experience of his family's ancestral home of Timbuctoo, New Jersey, one of the earliest land-owning free black communities in America, now a revered archeological site. We are honored to have all of their contributions.

It's only because of these folks that you hold in your hands this ode to African American foodways. More than that, it is a keepsake—one we hope you'll pass down for many generations.

— Ramin Ganeshram,
NOVEMBER 2010

Endnotes

Introduction: Stirring the Melting Pot

1. "goober," *Dictionary.com, 2009.* http://dictionary.reference.com/browse/goober (accessed: February 25, 2009).

2. "gumbo." *Dictionary.com, 2009.* http://dictionary.reference.com/browse/gumbo (accessed: February 25, 2009).

3. http://library.thinkquest.org/16645/the_people/ethnic_bantu.shtml

4. Robert L. Hall, "Food Crops, Medicinal Plants and the Atlantic Slave Trade" in Anne L. Bower, ed., *African American Foodways: Explorations of History and Culture* (Champaign: University of Illinois Press, 2007), 17.

5. Judith A. Carney, *Black Rice: The African Origins of Rice Cultivation in the Americas.* (Cambridge, MA: Harvard University Press, 2001).

6. James A. McMillin, *The Final Victims: Foreign Slave Trade to North America 1783–1810.* (Columbia, SC: University of South Carolina Press, 2004).

7. www.ers.usda.gov/Briefing/Rice/2008baseline.htm

8. Nell I. Painter, *Creating Black Americans: African American History and its Meanings, 1619 to Present* (New York, NY: Oxford University Press, 2006).

9. Mason I. Lowance, Jr., ed., "Population Statistics from the U.S. Census for 1790–1860" in *A House Divided: The Antebellum Slavery Debates in America, 1776–1865* (Princeton, NJ: Princeton University Press, 2003), 6.

10. Jessica B. Harris, "Same Boat, Different Stops: An African Atlantic Culinary Journey" in *African Roots/American Cultures: Africa in the Creation of the Americas,* Sheila Walker, ed., (Lanham, MD: Rowman & Littlefield Publishers, Inc., 2001), 172.

11. Joseph E. Holloway, "What Africa Has Given American Culture: African Continuities in the North American Diaspora" in *Africanisms in American Culture,* Joseph E. Holloway, ed. (Bloomington, IN: Indiana University Press, 2005), 48.

12. http://www.africanfoods.co.uk/gari.html

13. http://www.congocookbook.com/staple_dish_recipes/fufu.html

14. William D. Pierson, *Black Legacy: America's Hidden Heritage* (The University of Massachusetts Press, 1993).

15. Thelma Wills Foote, *Black and White Manhattan: The History of Racial Formation in Colonial New York City* (New York, NY: Oxford University Press, 2004).

16. http://www.slavenorth.com/massemancip.htm

17. http://www.slavenorth.com/nyemancip.htm

18. Eric Arnesen, ed., "Domestic Service" in *Encyclopedia of U.S. Labor and Working-Class History, Volume 1* (New York, NY: Routledge Taylor & Frances Group, 2007), 372–373.

19. http://www.cooks.com/rec/search/0,1-0,monkey_bread,FF.html

Chapter 3: Presidential Cooks

20. Alonzo Fields, *My 21 Years in the White House* (Greenwich, CT: Fawcett Publications, 1961), 58–9; New York Times, Proquest Historical Newspapers, July 28, 1935, 1.

21. "New White House Chef," *Chicago Tribune,* April 19, 1897, 5. (Proquest Historical Newspapers).

22. "White House Cook Dead," *Washington Post,* February 12, 1918, 9. (Proquest Historical Newspapers).

23. "Wilson Will Enjoy Southern Cooking," *New York Times,* January 26, 1913, 14 (Proquest Historical Newspapers); "Corn Pone Popular Food," Los Angeles Times, March 21, 1915, III20. (Proquest Historical Newspapers).

24. "Taft Keeps a Bachelor's Hall," *Baltimore Sun,* July 14, 1909, 2. (Proquest Historical Newspapers).

25. Randall Bennett Woods, LBJ: *Architect of American Ambition* (Boston, MA: Harvard University Press, 2007) 411–12.

26. Ernest May and Timothy J. Naftali, eds., *The Presidential Recordings: Lyndon Baines Johnson* (New York, NY: W. W. Norton & Company, 2001), 211.

27. Frank X. Tolbert, *A Bowl of Red* (Dallas, TX: Taylor Publishing Company, 1988), 12.

28. Francis Edward Abernethy, ed., *2001: A Texas Folklore Odyssey* (Denton, TX: Publication of the Texas Folklore Society LVIII, University of North Texas Press, 2001), 220–21.

29. Edwin Morris Betts and James Adam Bear, Jr., eds., *The Family Letters of Thomas Jefferson* (Charlottesville, Virginia: Thomas Jefferson Memorial Foundation by the University Press of Virginia, 1986), 238–39.

Index

About the Editors

Source: The Henderson Group

Jeff Henderson grew up in Southern California and was born into a family of great cooks. Nevertheless, it was only many years later while he was incarcerated that he was bitten by the culinary bug and discovered one of his greatest passions—cooking. Once released, he embarked on a career as a chef. Working his way up from dishwasher to line cook, he became the first African American to be named chef de cuisine at Caesar's Palace in Las Vegas and later executive chef at Cafe Bellagio. His first book, the memoir *Cooked*, was a *New York Times* bestseller and is slated to become a feature film. He hosted The Chef Jeff Project, a docu-reality series on the Food Network, and is the author of *Chef Jeff Cooks*. Jeff lives in Las Vegas with his wife, Stacy, and their four children. To learn more about Chef Jeff, visit **www.chefjeffcooked.com.**

● ● ●

Ramin Ganeshram was born in New York City to a Trinidadian father and Iranian mother. She is an award-winning journalist and professionally trained chef whose work has appeared in *Saveur*, epicurious.com, *National Geographic Traveler*, *O*, and more. She is the author of *Sweet Hands: Island Cooking from Trinidad & Tobago* and *Stir It Up!*, a culinary novel for middle-grade readers.

Source: Jean Paul Vellotti

SmileyBooks Titles of Related Interest

DVD

STAND: a film by Tavis Smiley

BOOKS

AMERICA I AM LEGENDS:
Rare Moments and Inspiring Words
Edited by SmileyBooks; foreword by Tavis Smiley

AMERICA I AM BLACKFACTS:
The Timelines of African American History 1601–2008
by Quintard Taylor

AMERICA I AM JOURNAL:
The African American Imprint
Edited by Clarence Reynolds

PEACE FROM BROKEN PIECES:
How to Get Through What You're Going Through
by Iyanla Vanzant

BRAINWASHED:
Challenging the Myth of Black Inferiority
by Tom Burrell

EVERYTHING I'M NOT MADE ME EVERYTHING I AM:
Discovering Your Personal Best
by Jeff Johnson

NEVER MIND SUCCESS . . . GO FOR GREATNESS!
The Best Advice I've Ever Received
by Tavis Smiley

CARD DECKS

EMPOWERMENT CARDS: A-50 CARD DECK
by Tavis Smiley

EMPOWERMENT CARDS FOR INSPIRED LIVING
by Tavis Smiley

Available at your local bookstore, or online through our distributor, Hay House, at www.hayhouse.com®

We hoped you enjoyed this SMILEYBOOKS publication.
If you would like to receive additional information, please contact:

SMILEYBOOKS

Distributed by:

Hay House, Inc.
P.O. Box 5100
Carlsbad, CA 92018-5100

(760) 431-7695 or (800) 654-5126
(760) 431-6948 (fax) or (800) 650-5115 (fax)
www.hayhouse.com® • www.hayfoundation.org

• • •

Published and distributed in Australia by:
Hay House Australia Pty. Ltd. • 18/36 Ralph St. • Alexandria NSW 2015
Phone: 612-9669-4299 • Fax: 612-9669-4144 • www.hayhouse.com.au

Published and distributed in the United Kingdom by:
Hay House UK, Ltd. • 292B Kensal Rd., London W10 5BE
Phone: 44-20-8962-1230 • Fax: 44-20-8962-1239 • www.hayhouse.co.uk

Published and distributed in the Republic of South Africa by:
Hay House SA (Pty), Ltd., P.O. Box 990, Witkoppen 2068
Phone/Fax: 27-11-467-8904 • info@hayhouse.co.za • www.hayhouse.co.za

Published and Distributed in India by:
Hay House Publishers India, Muskaan Complex, Plot No. 3, B-2, Vasant Kunj,
New Delhi 110 070 • *Phone: 91-11-4176-1620 • Fax: 91-11-4176-1630 • www.hayhouse.co.in*

Distributed in Canada by:
Raincoast • 9050 Shaughnessy St., Vancouver, B.C. V6P 6E5
Phone: (604) 323-7100 • Fax: (604) 323-2600

• • •